Marlboro Nights
Come to where the smoking was

I0472102

Documenting the ban on smoking in public

by Garry Cook

ISBN-ISBN-13: 978-1477608142
ISBN-10: 1477608141

www.gazcook.com
www.lovetown.eu

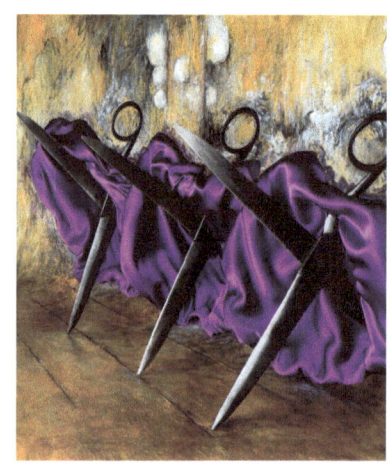

7mg TAR 0·7mg NICOTINE
PROTECT CHILDREN:
DON'T MAKE THEM BREATHE YOUR SMOKE
Health Departments' Chief Medical Officers

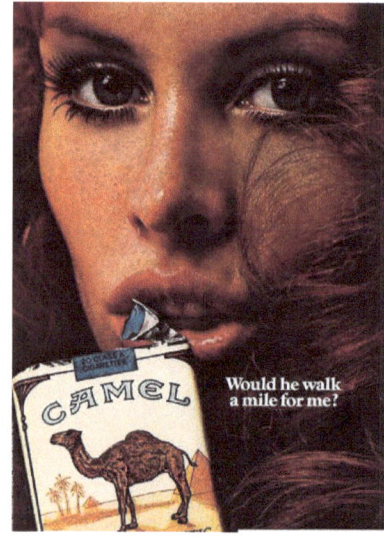

Would he walk
a mile for me?

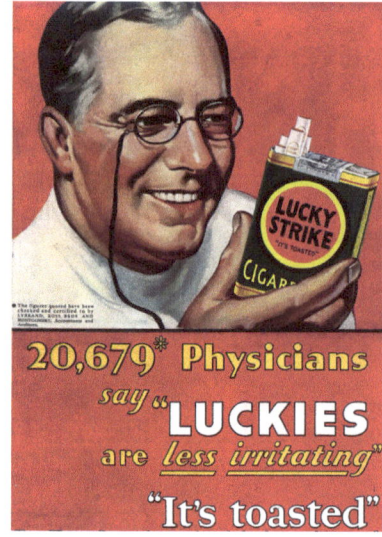

20,679* Physicians
say "LUCKIES
are *less irritating*"

"It's toasted"

THESE photos are part of a documentary project on the ban on smoking in public places which became law in England on July 1, 2007.

This book captures smokers in social situations before the ban came into force. And the story continued as the smokers were forced to go outside.

In the build-up to the smoking switch-off I visited pubs, nightclubs, working men's clubs, social clubs, bingo halls and shisha cafes.

Taking place over several months, the project was in many ways unique. After all, there is no other photography project you can do in which you can passively kill yourself.

I particularly enjoyed the shisha bars in Rusholme, Manchester, where I found people highly accommodating and friendly. While I'm glad of the ban for purely personal reasons – no more smokey clothes – I do think it is a shame that many shisha bars have closed.

Apart from being culturally important to the Asian community, they exist only for smoking and I can differentiate between smoking in a shisha cafe and smoking in a pub.

Some nights were longer than others taking photographs of smokers. And during every one of them I was asked several times, 'what do you think of the smoking ban?'.

I tried always to give a non-decisive, diplomatic answer. I was documenting a social-issues subject without bias…

But now, five years on, I can lie back, smell my clothes and think, 'thank god I don't have to put with that anymore'.

How did we put up with it all for so long? How did I, for most of my life, stomach not just smoking in pubs and nightclubs but smoking on buses, on trains and even, in my younger years, at the barbers?

I can't quite believe this was acceptable.

Just five years after the event and some of these images have a surreal feeling; nostalgia for a time now consigned to history. Today, some of these images are as peculiar as photos of old buses or crowds of the working-classes all wearing hats.

Smoking in pubs and nightclubs was accepted as normal. It was just how life was.

If, on a Sunday morning, you dared to put on a coat or a pair of jeans you had worn the night before, the smell of dirty smoke would cling to you. Now that

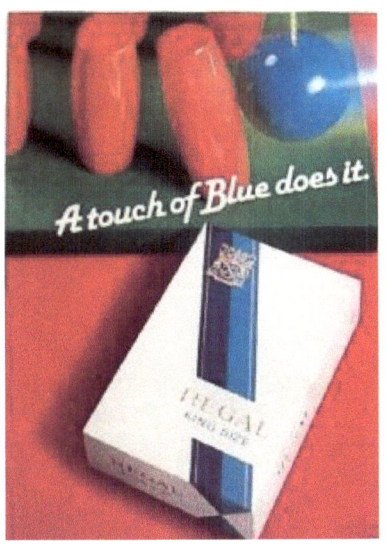 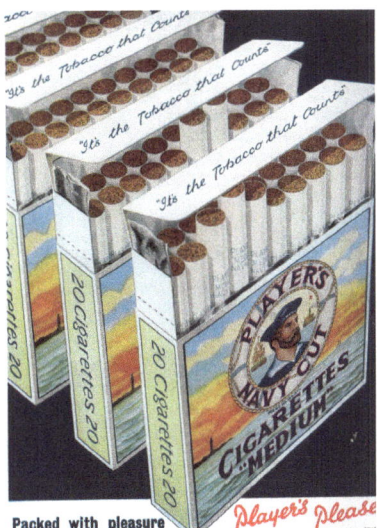 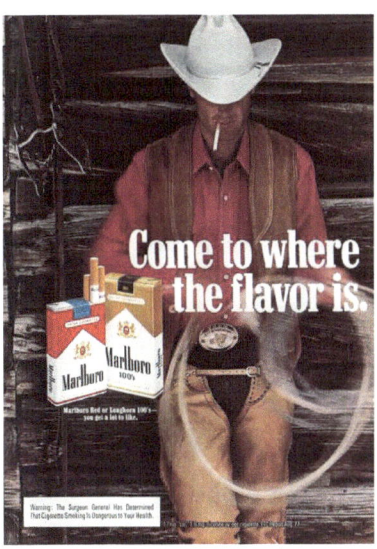

feeling is some distant memory. Go into a smoke-filled room today and you get an immediate feeling of repulsion – yet smoke was something I had hardly noticed for almost all of my life.

I don't miss smoking indoors and I don't think a ban on smoking in public places has repressed, taken away human rights or in any way infringed upon anyone's civil liberties.

Those who vigorously fought the ban, such as Blackpool licensee Hamish Howitt whose happy Scots Bar is featured in this book, did so primarily because it is human nature to oppose change. We are creatures of habit and for centuries, in pubs, the habit has been to smoke and drink.

Both habits are not good for our health but the big difference is smoking does not just affect the health of the smoker. Those surrounding the cigarettes are also affected.

That said, you can't deny the huge impact the ban on smoking has had on the pub trade. Hundreds of pubs have closed in Britain since the summer watershed of 2007. This is not coincidence.

Town and city centres were noticeably less busy in the months after the ban. I don't think they have ever recovered. Bingo halls have also suffered, with record numbers of closures across Britain since the ban was introduced.

Sad though this is, I don't think it is a good argument to allow smoking in public places just to keep these venues going.

There may well be an argument to allow venues to decide to remain smoke friendly – especially in the case of the hubbly bubbly and shisha cafes – but ultimately an outright ban is the right decision, for everyone's health.

I am old enough to remember smoking in offices, I remember every house I ever visited having ash trays all over the place. You don't see this anymore and I am glad.

Another question I was frequently asked during my stalking of smokers was, 'Do you smoke?'

The answer is simple: Never. Though after those countless long nights with a wide-angle lens shoved into people's smoky faces I felt like a twenty-a-day man.

Those days are over and I'm delighted.

June 4, 2012

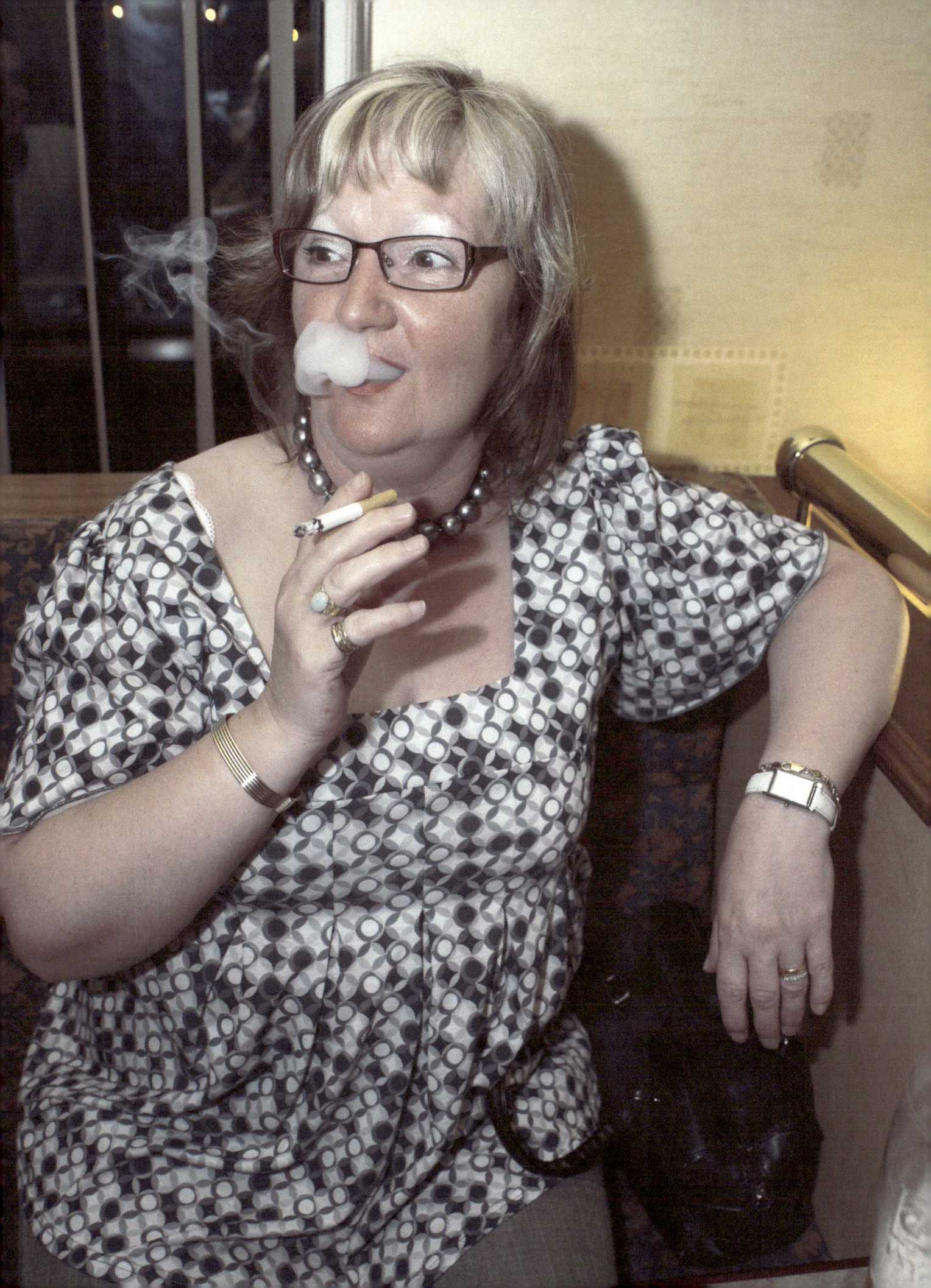

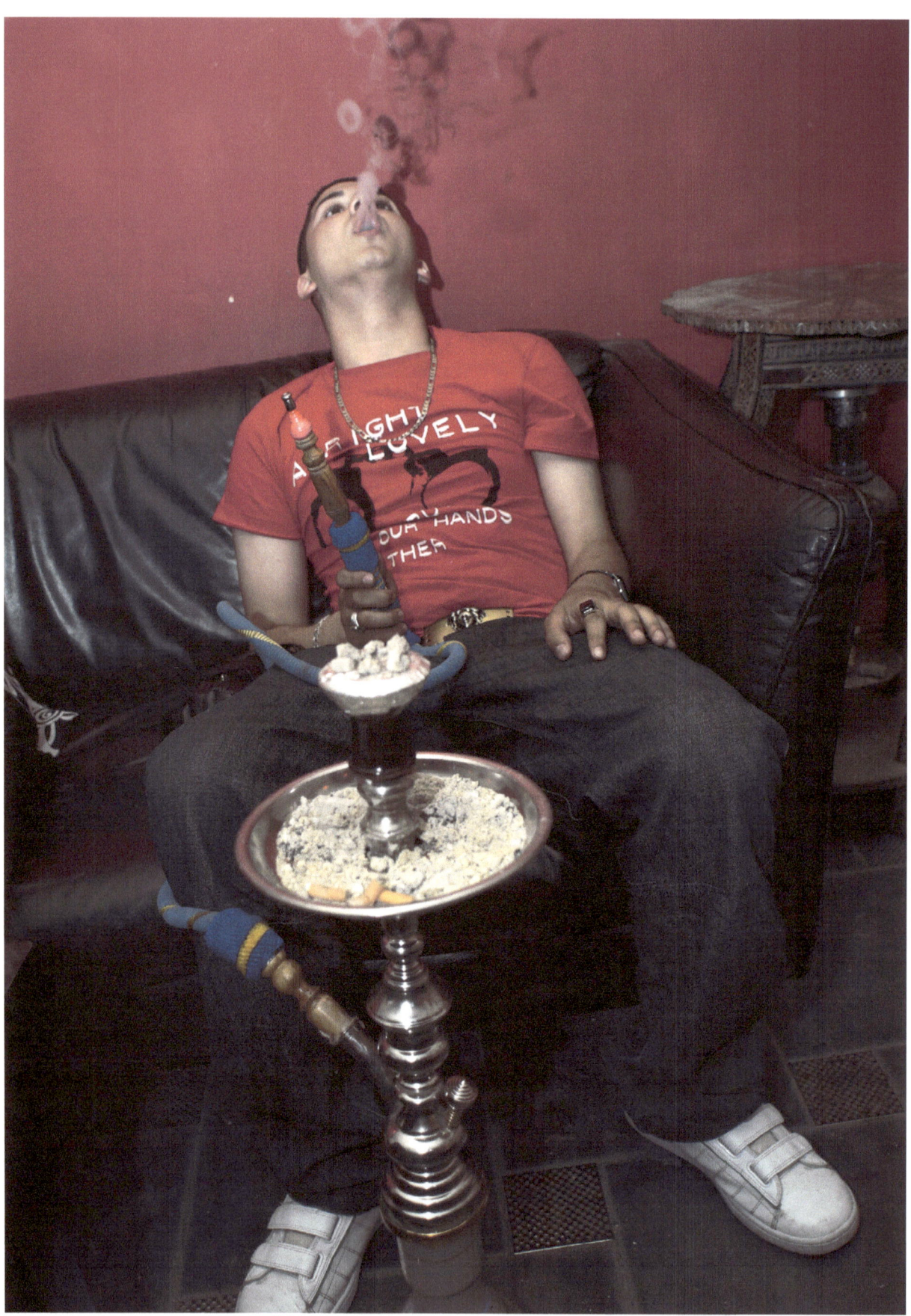

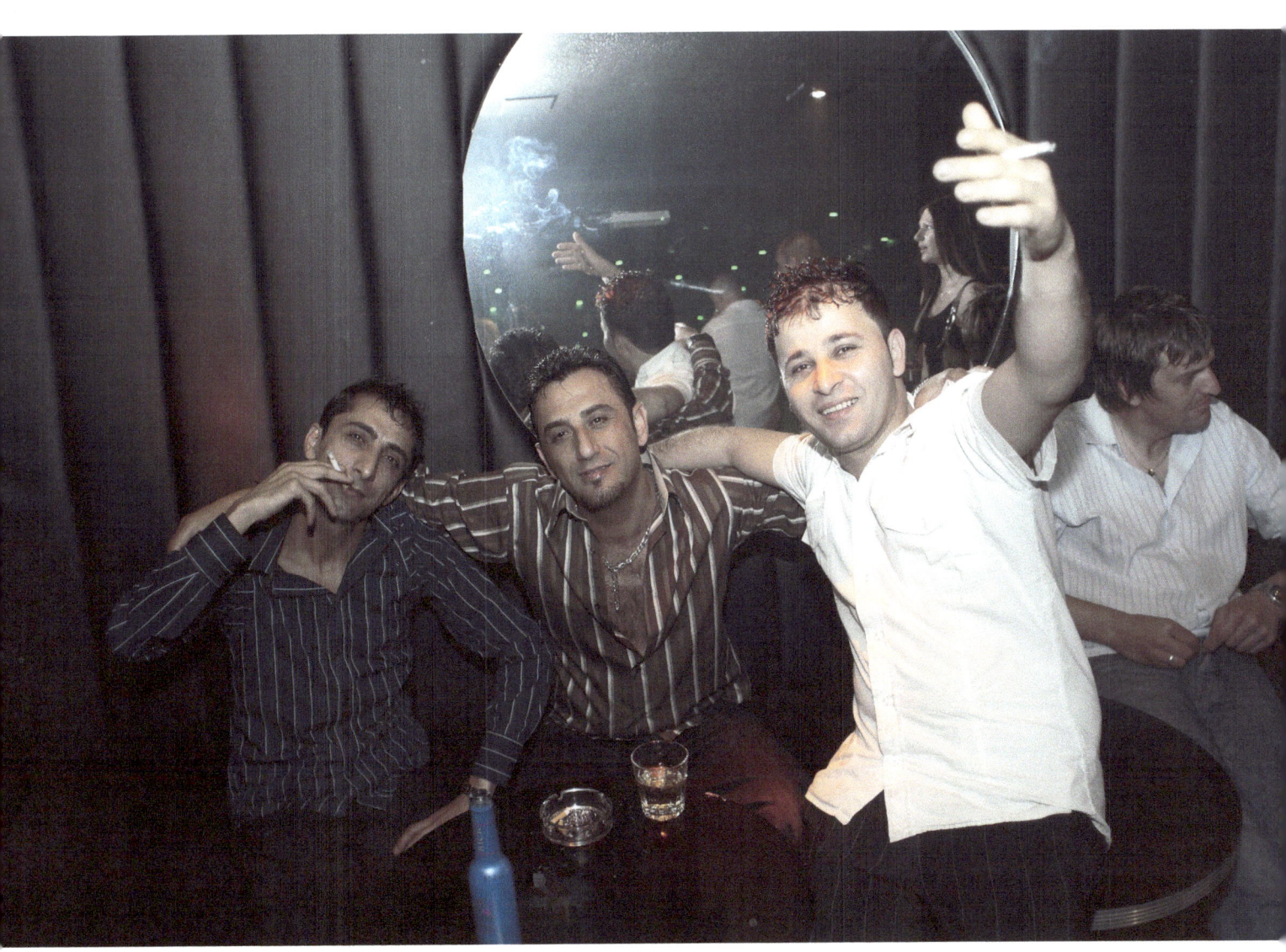

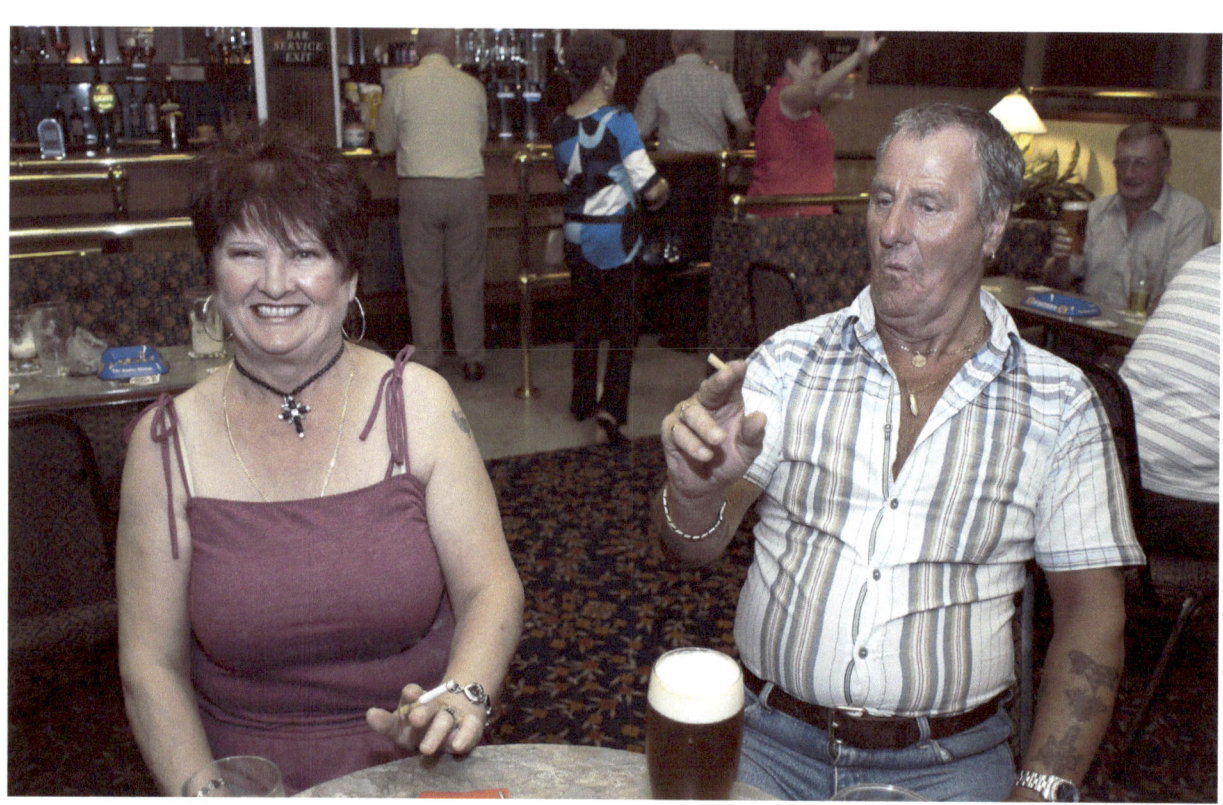

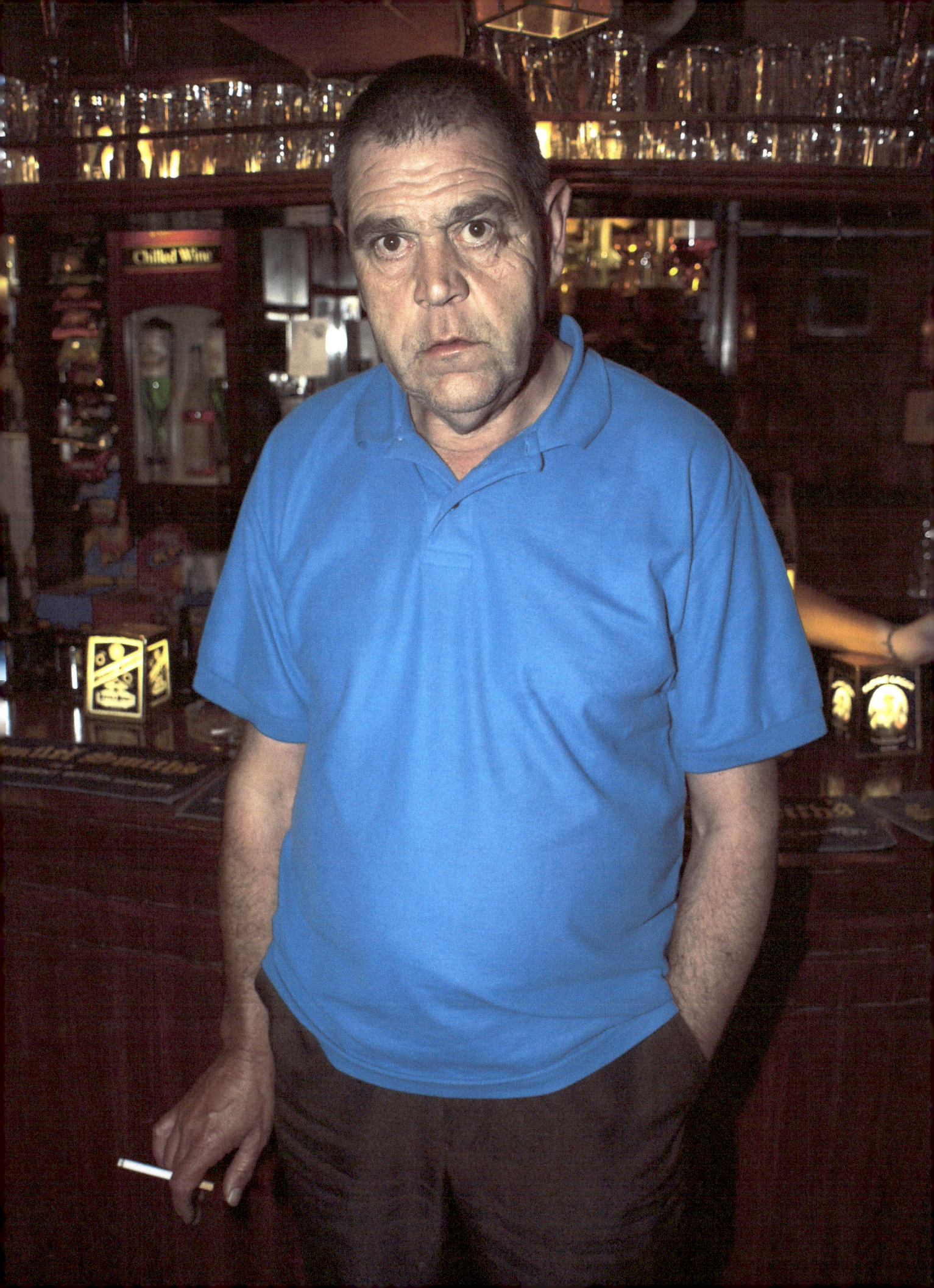

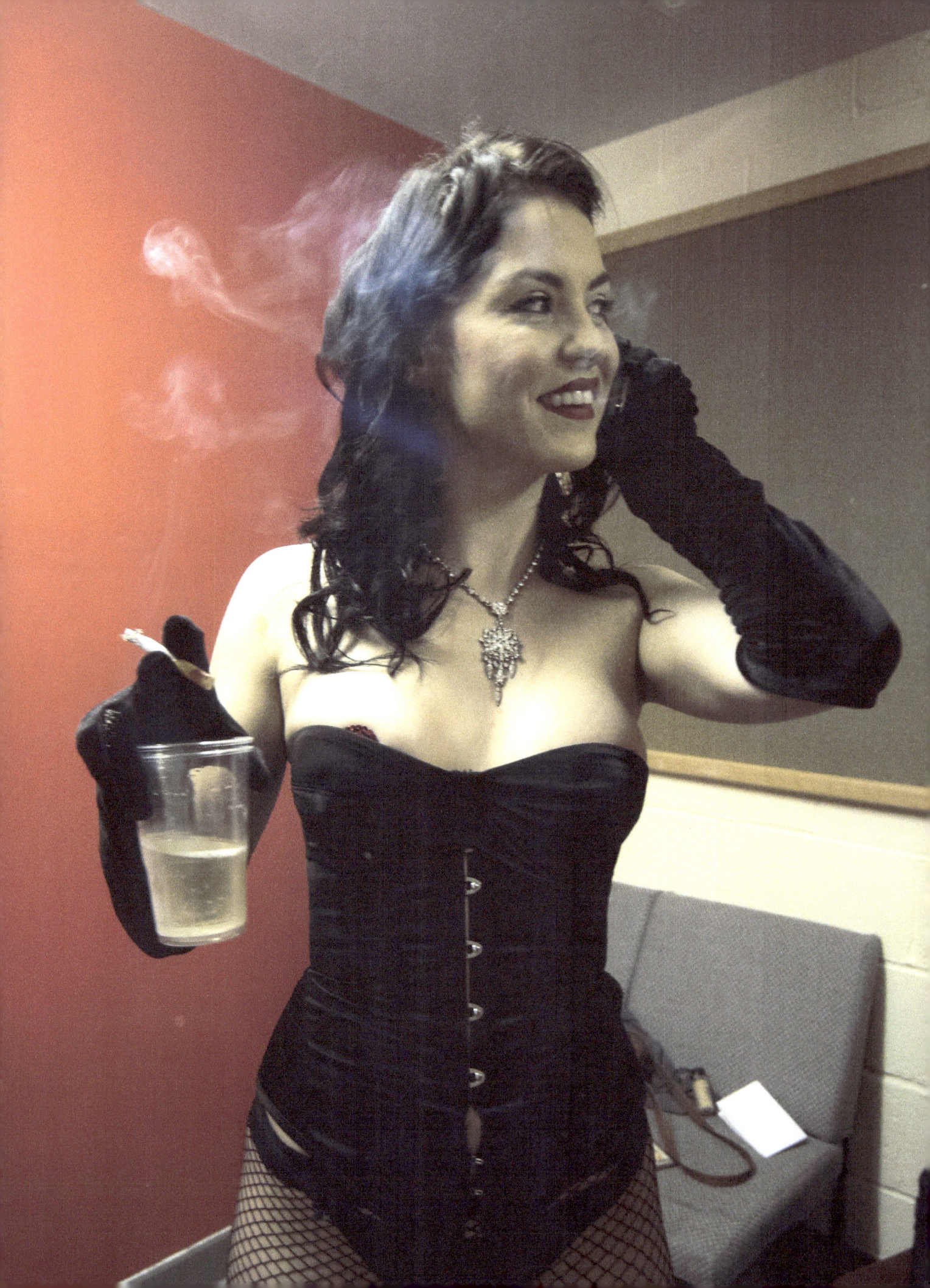

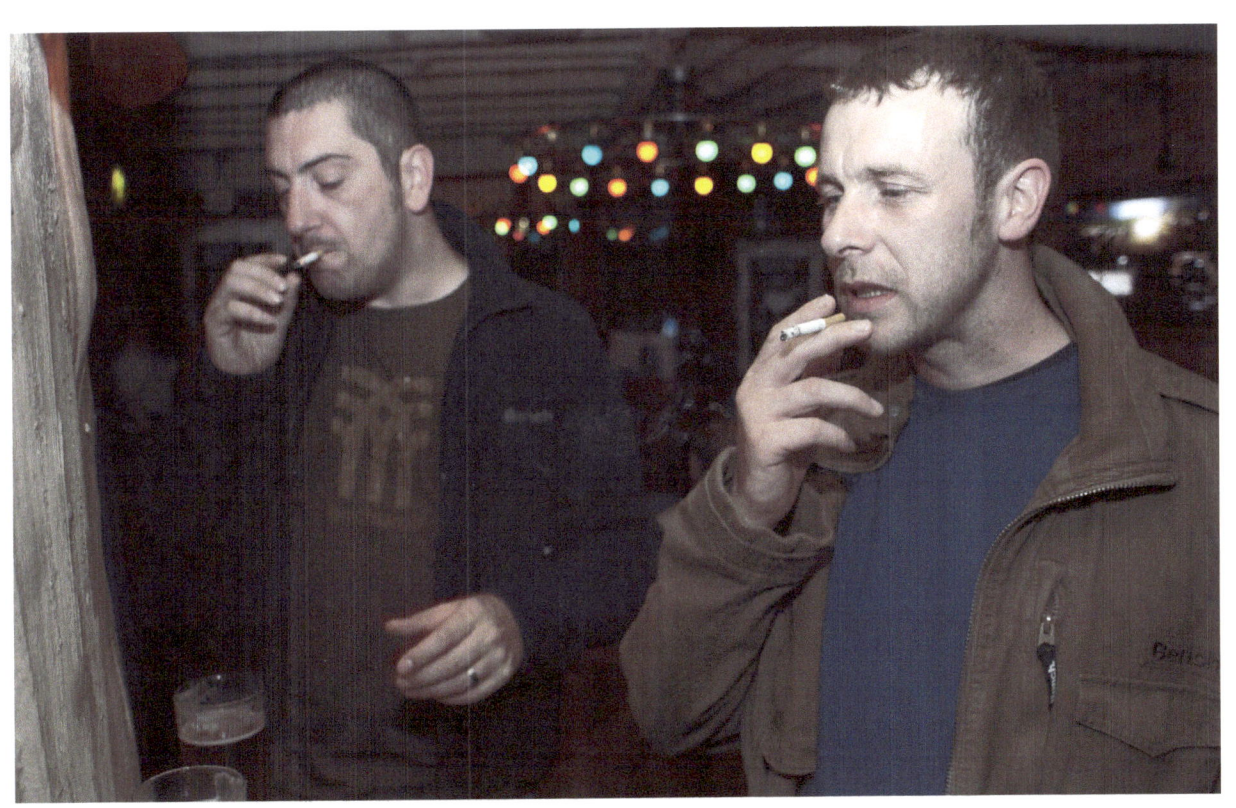

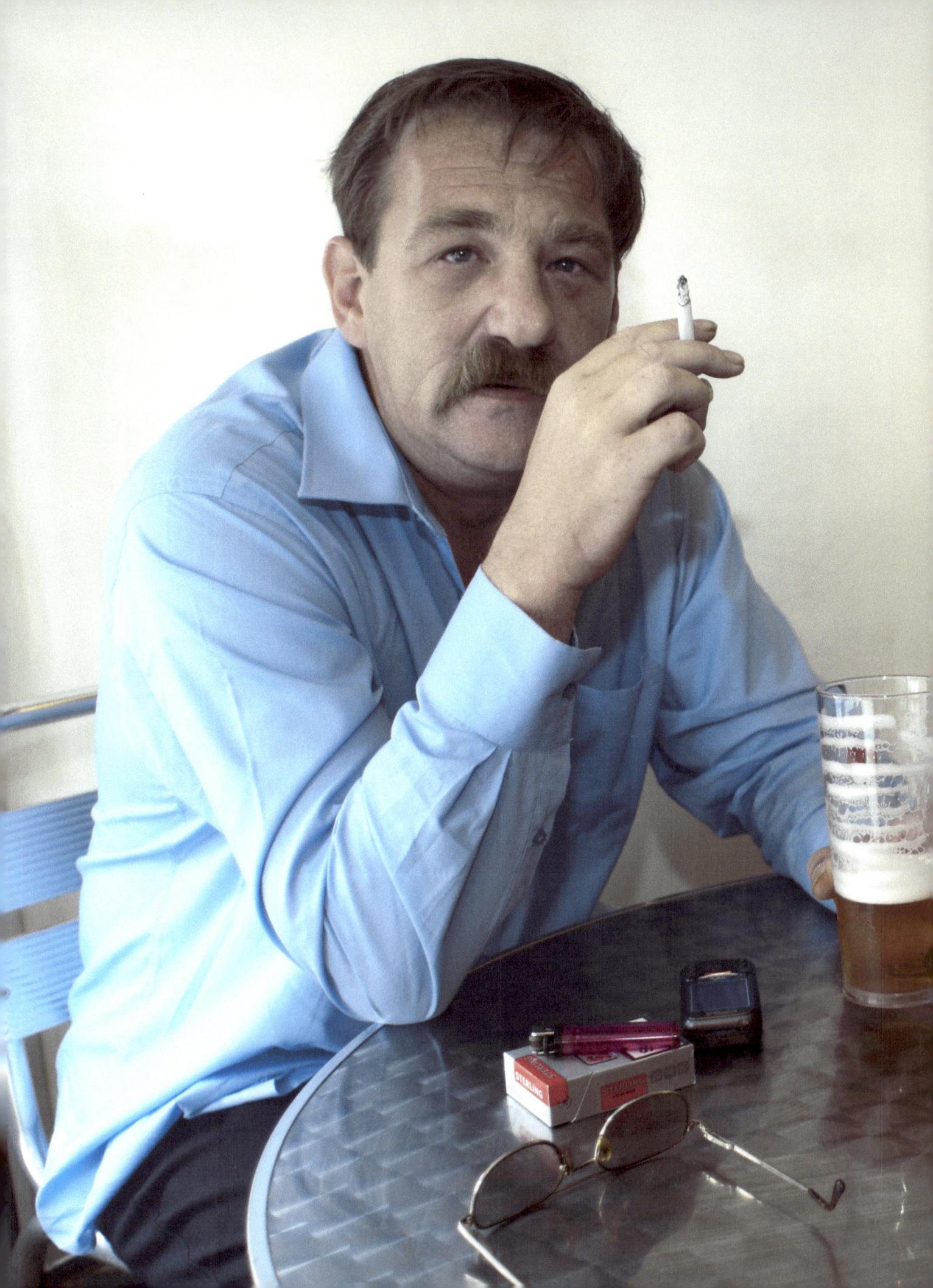

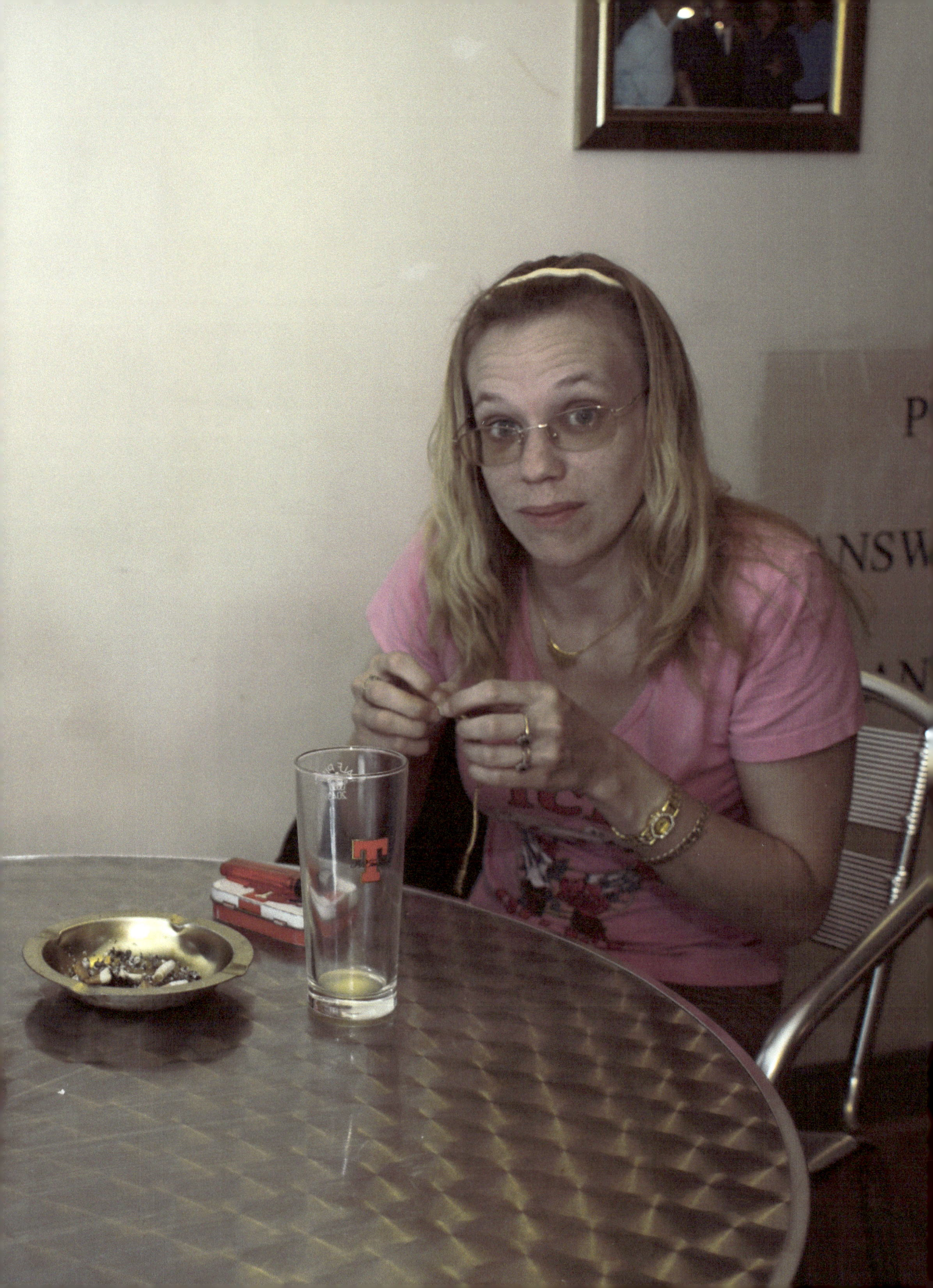

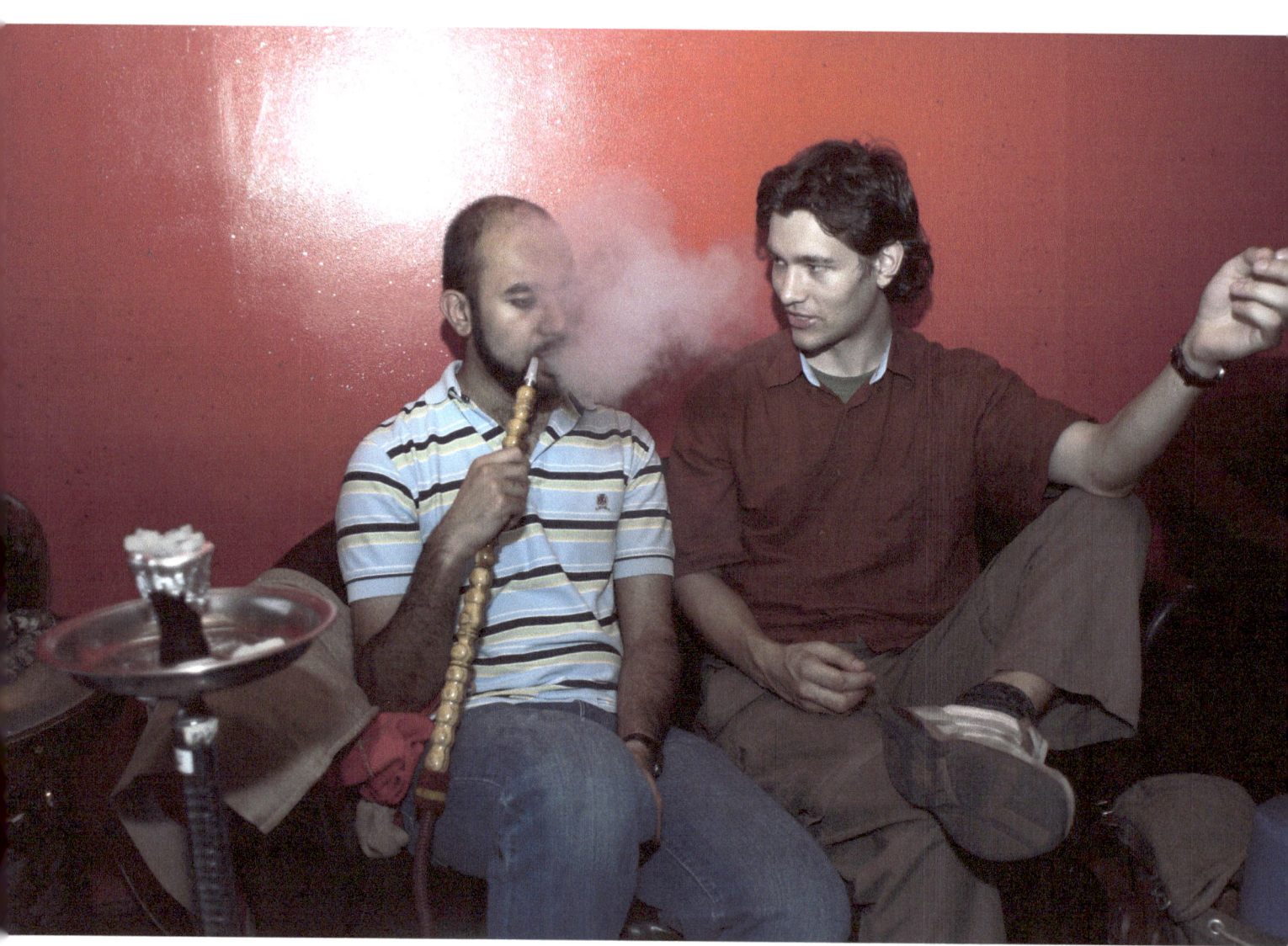

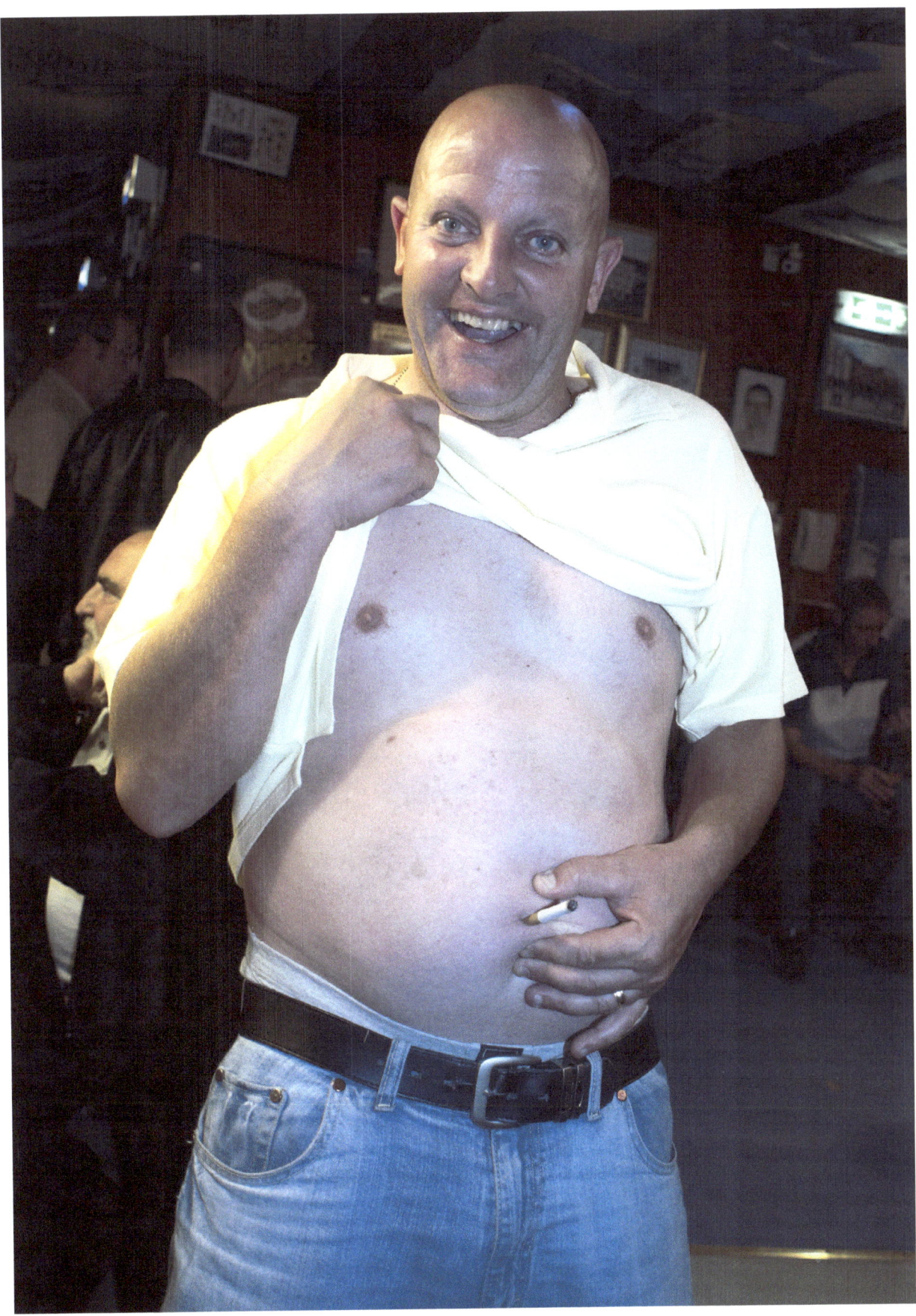

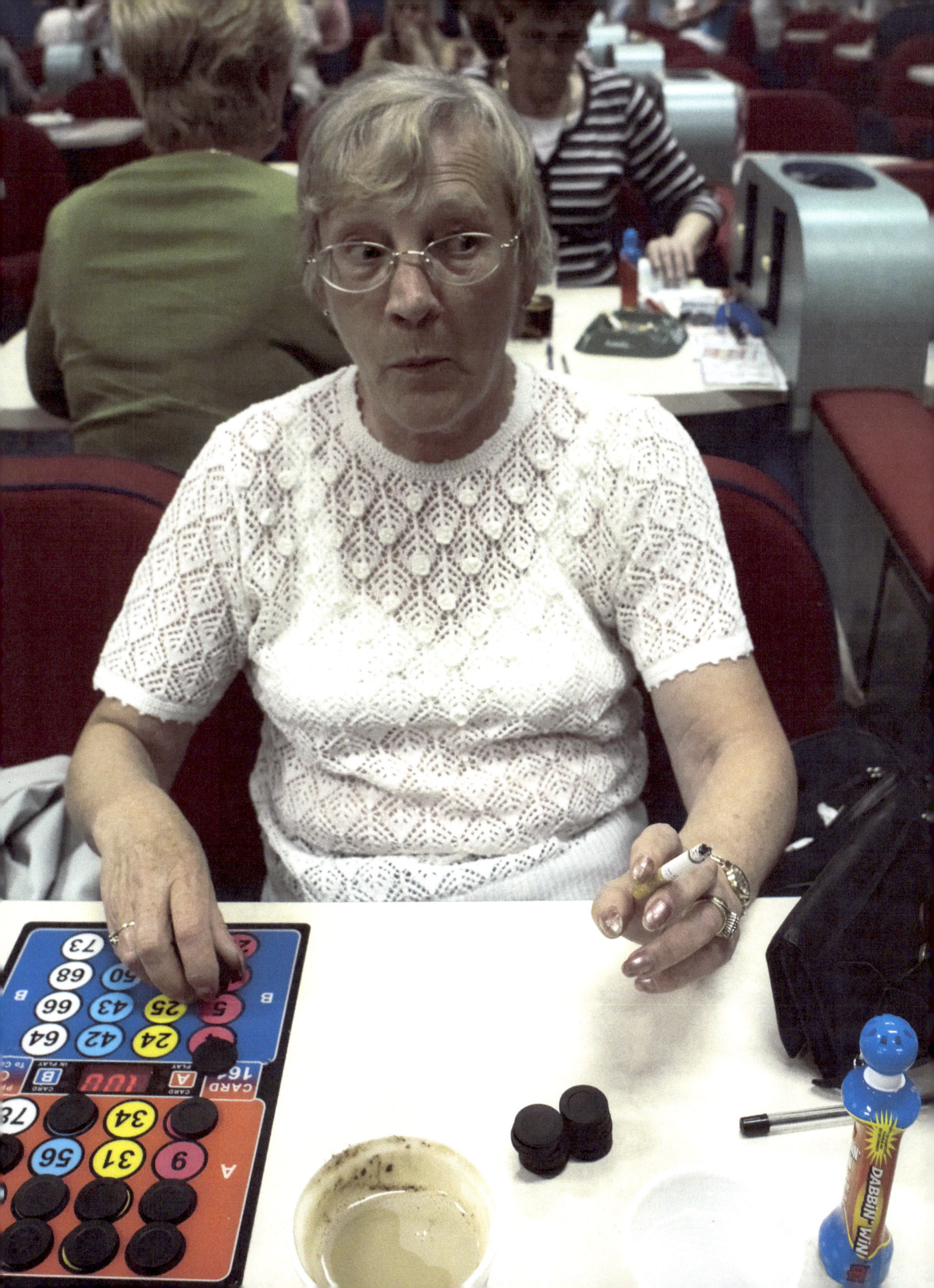

DOCUMENT, not comment – that's what I say when I'm challenged over why I'm taking photographs. And believe me, I get challenged a lot.

Last night I got two 'f*** offs' and one 'you're corrupt' (actually the second time for that one, though it was by the same man). No 'scums' though, so it was a fairly positive night.

Mind you, I was in Blackpool.

June 2, 2007

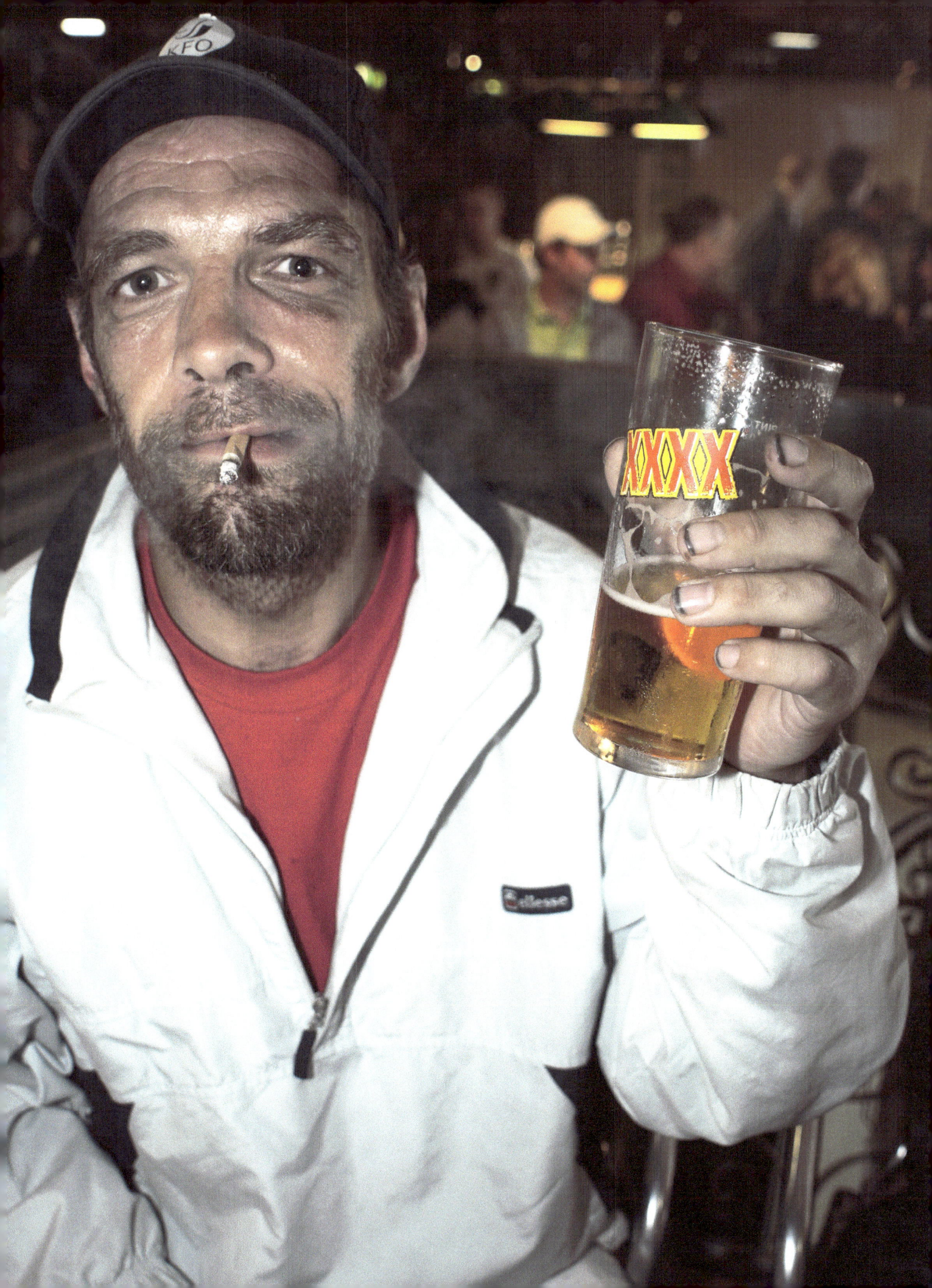

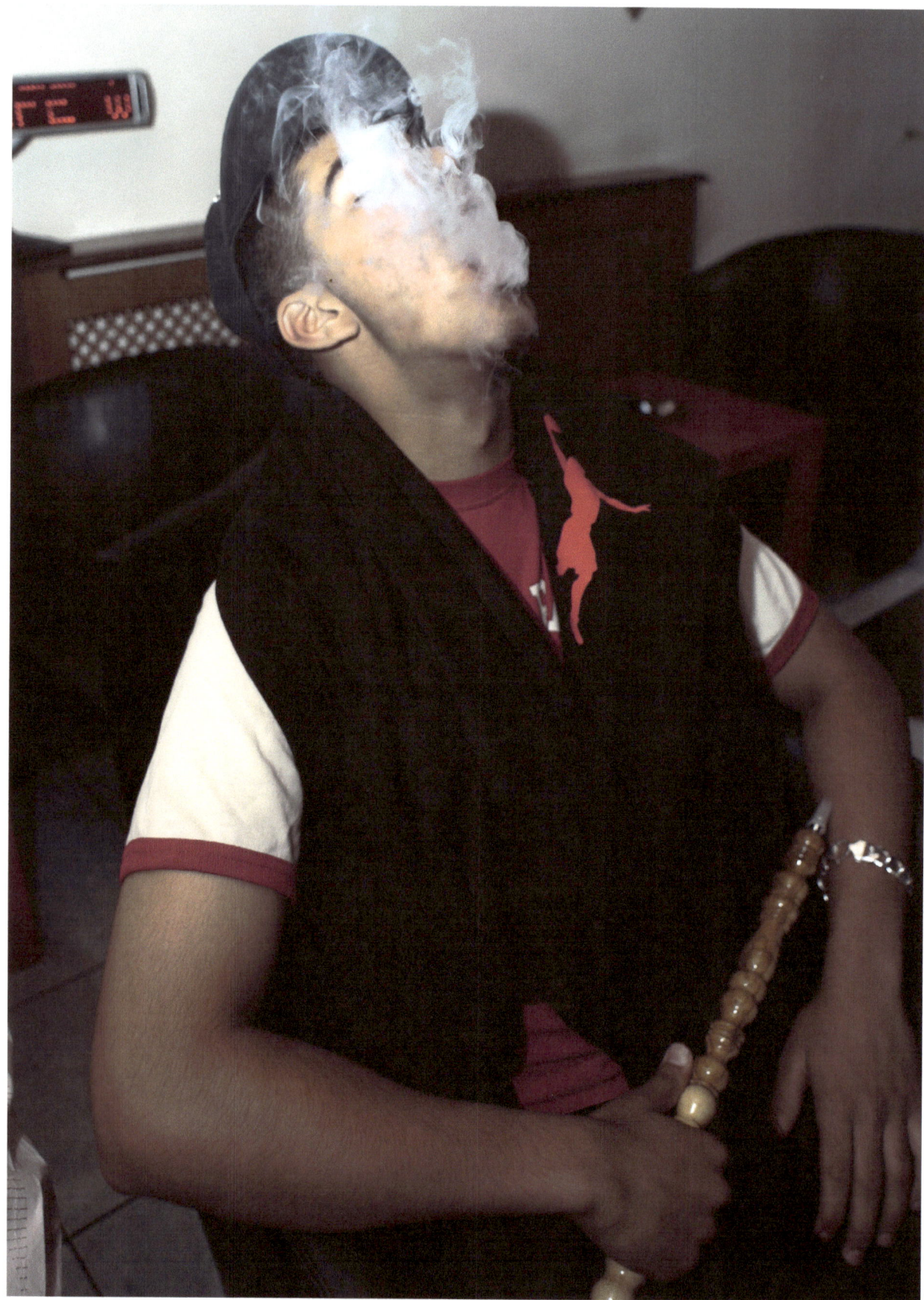

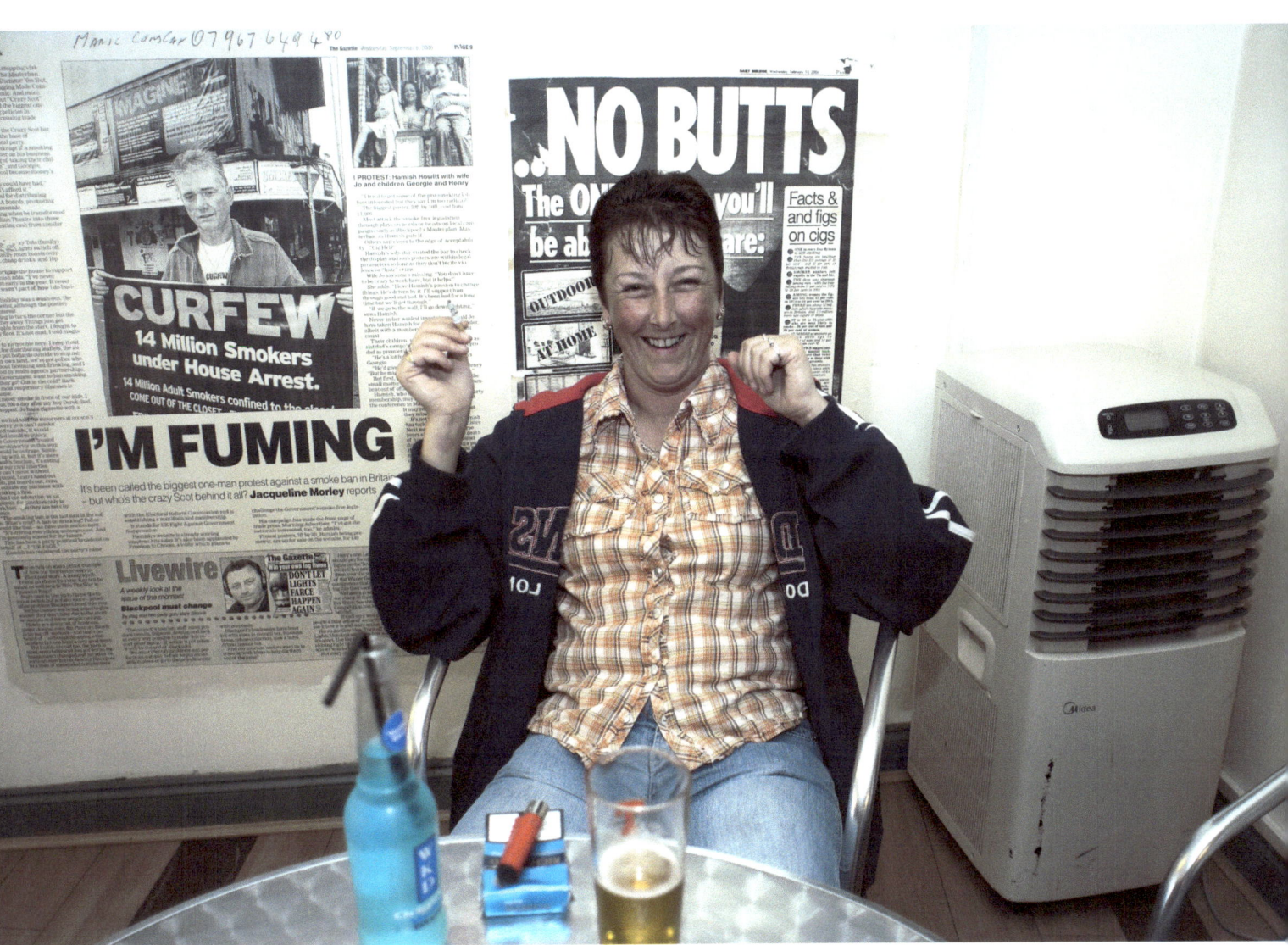

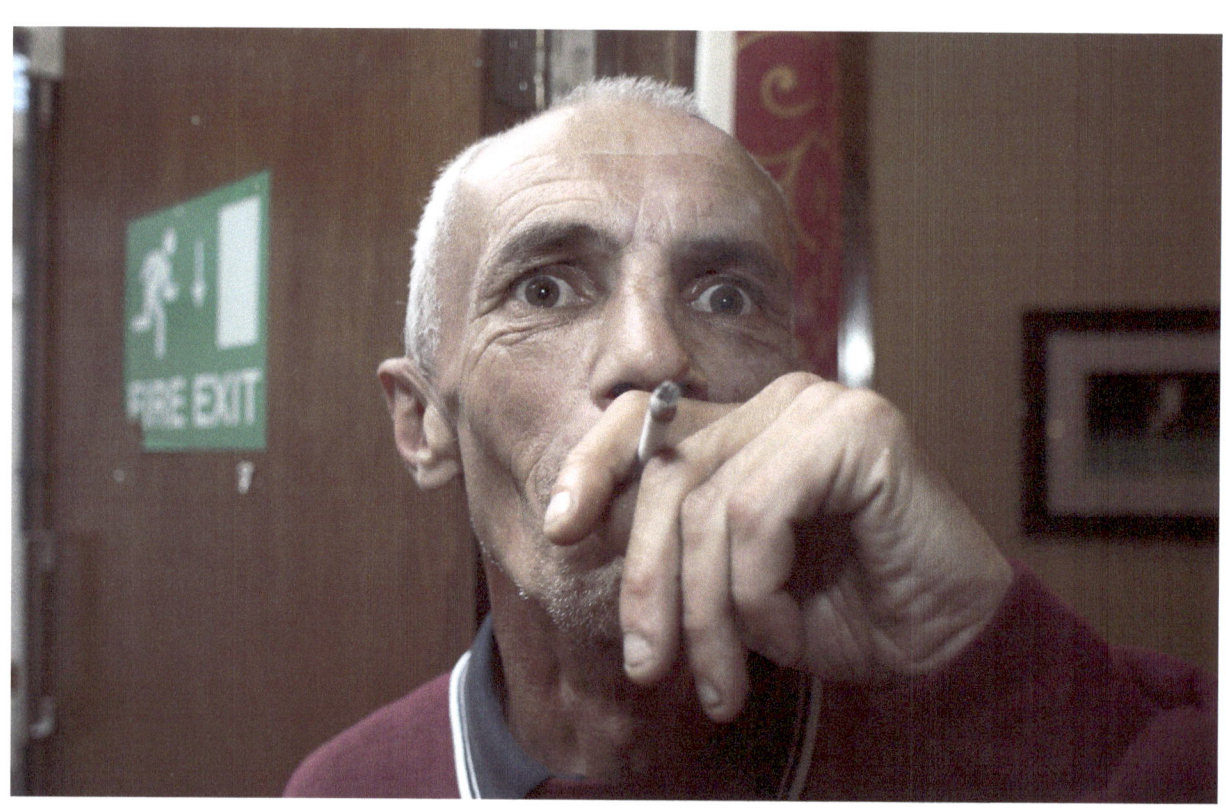

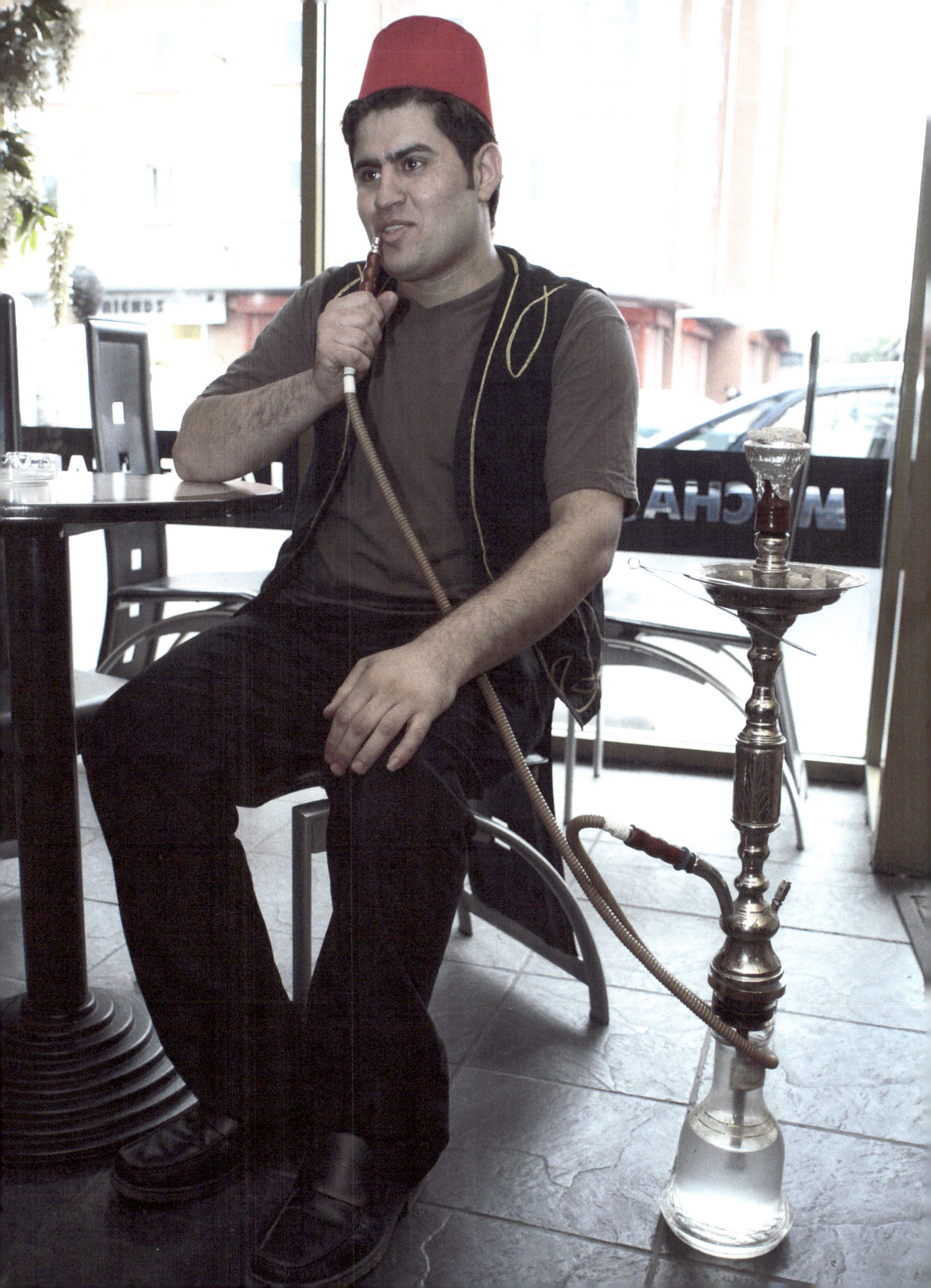

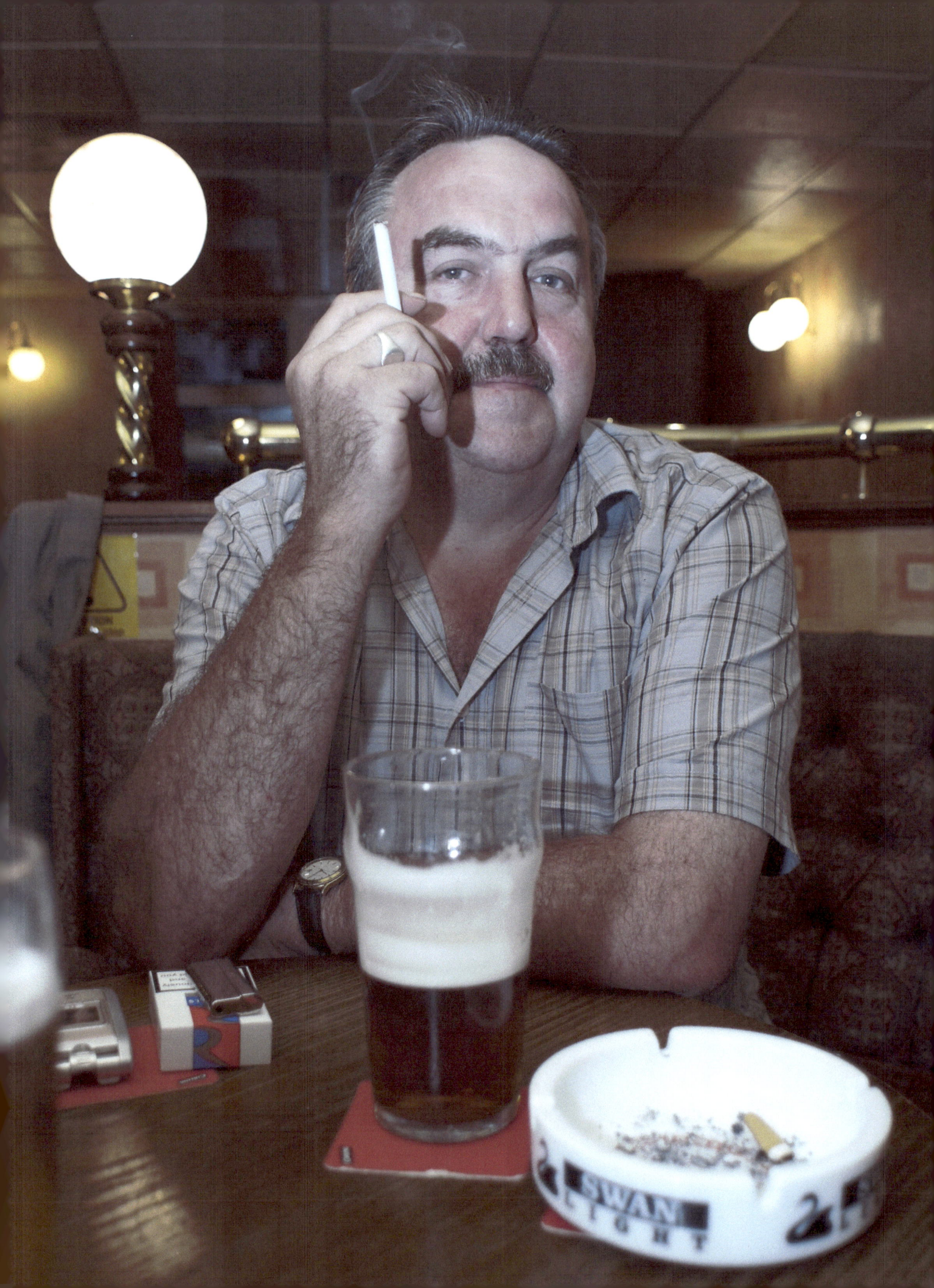

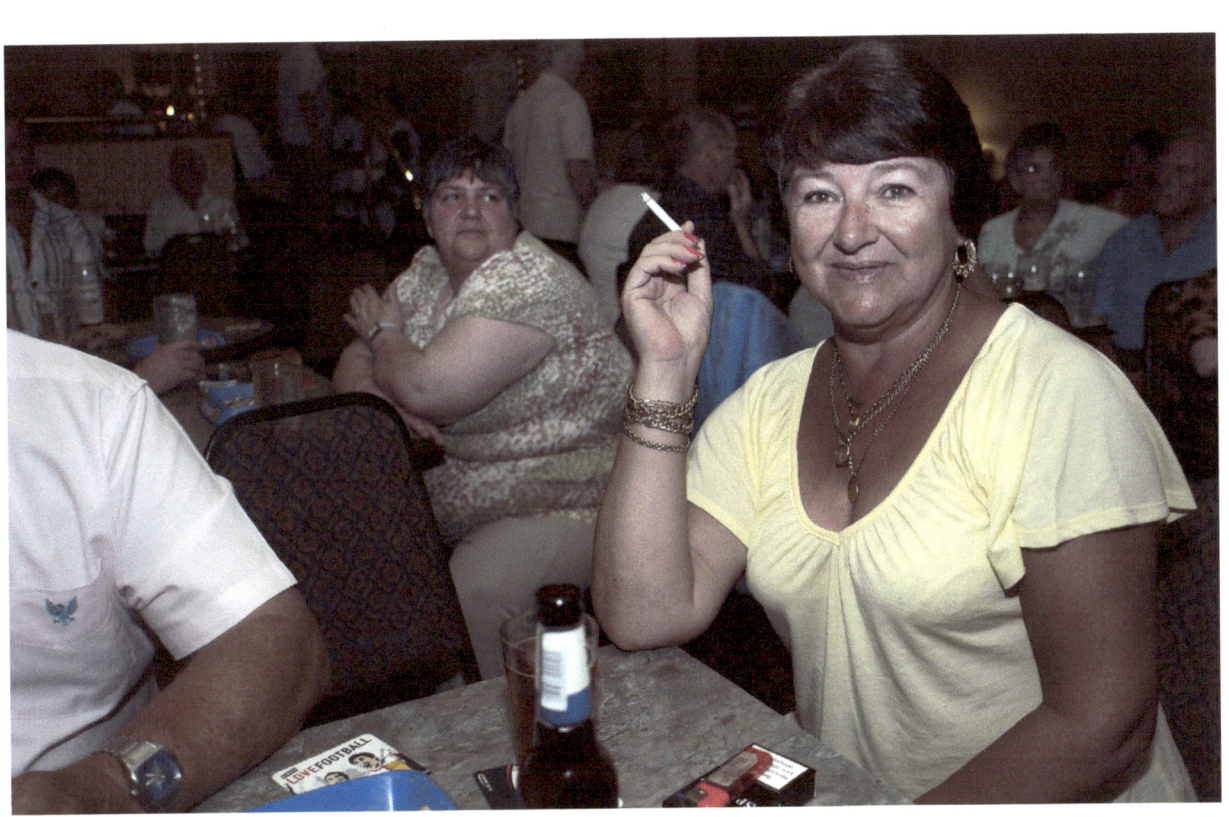

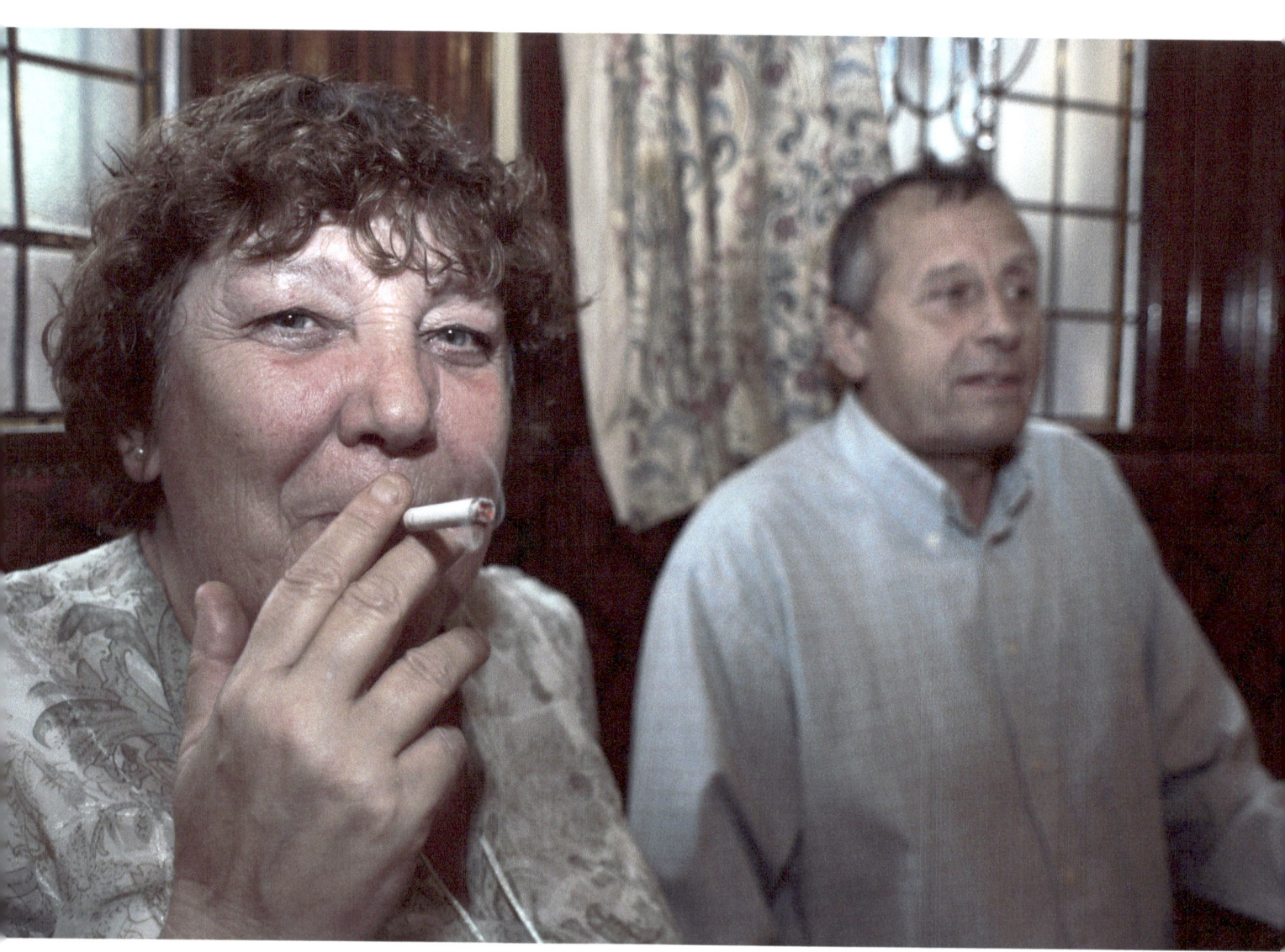

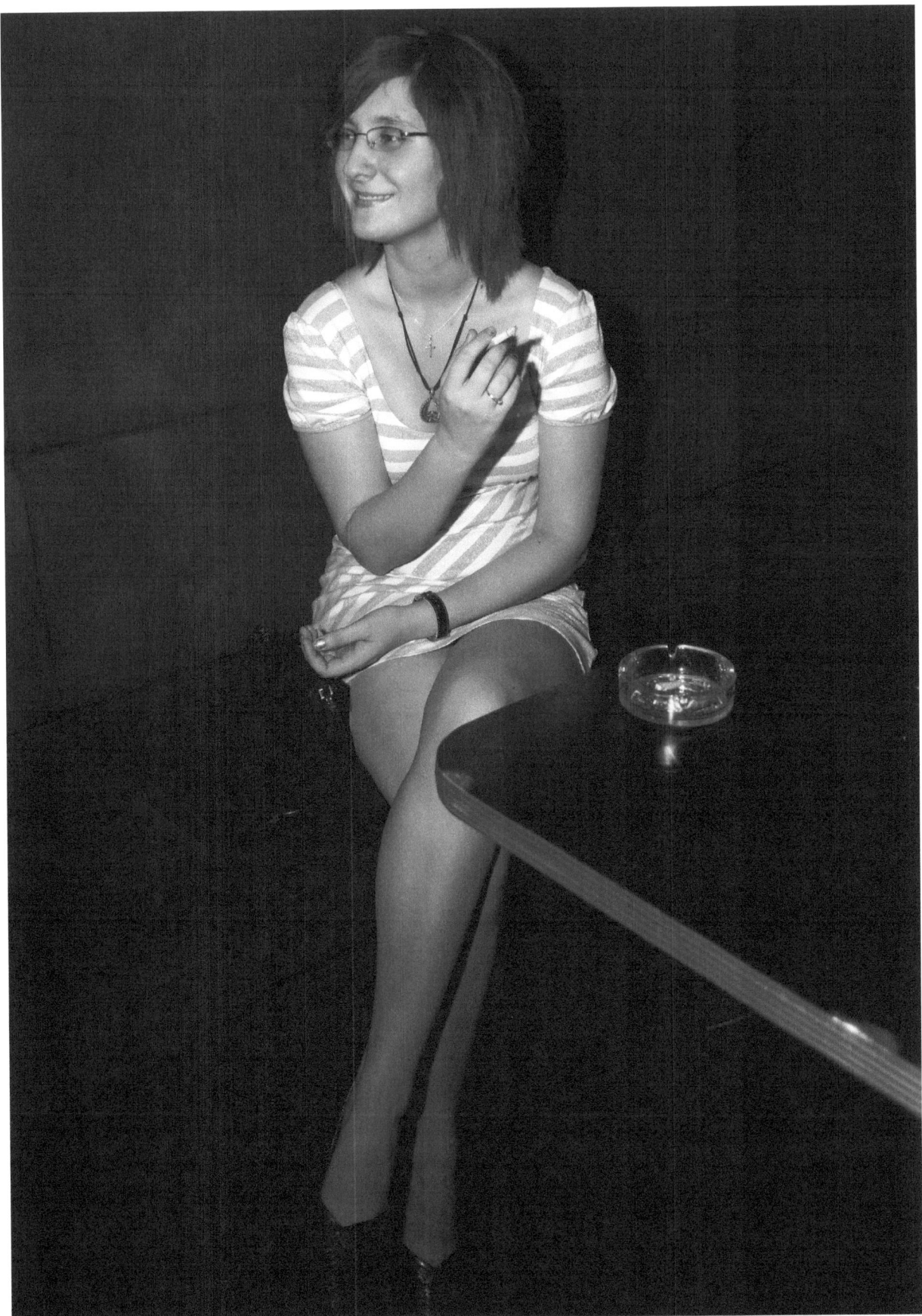

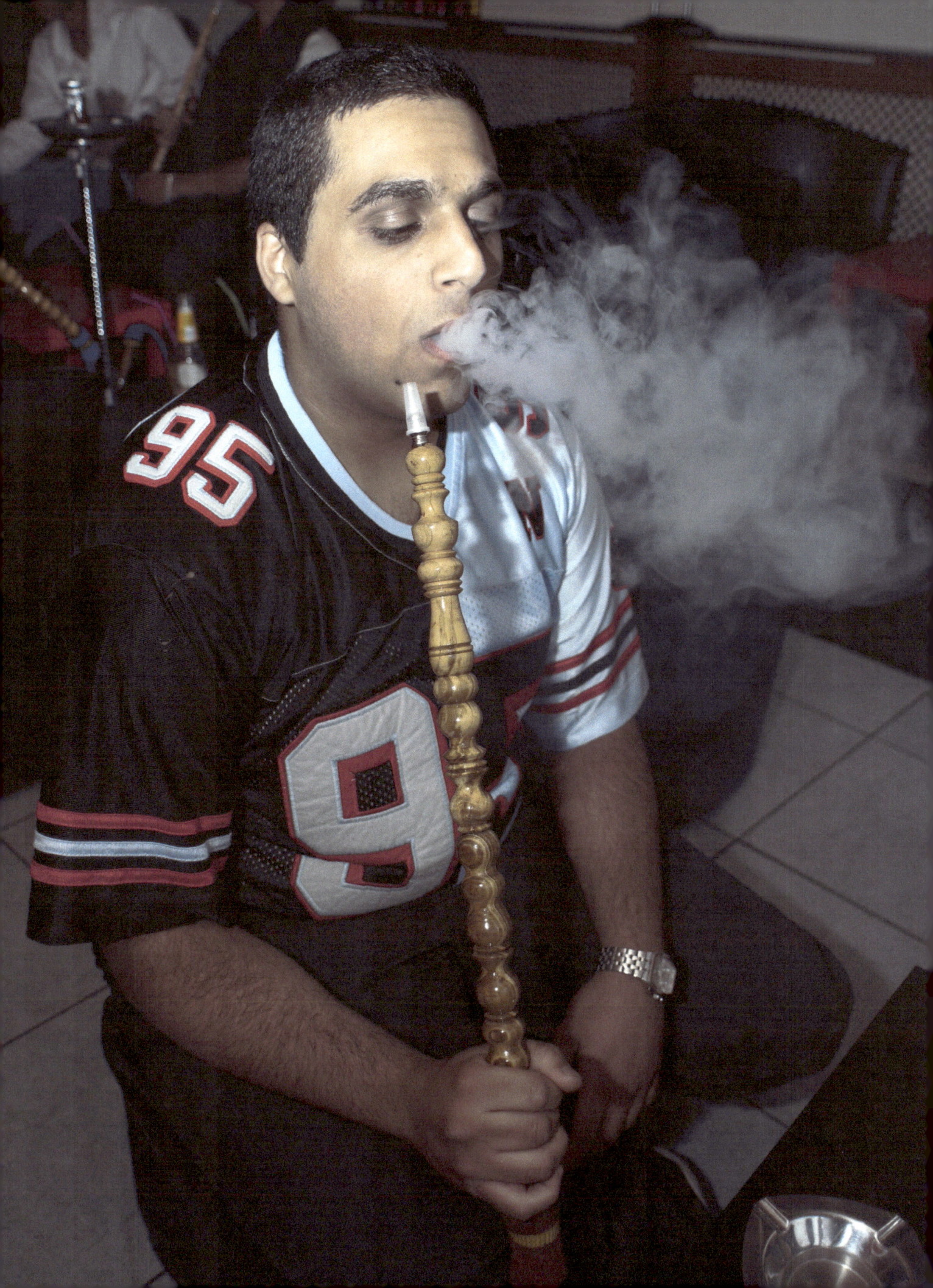

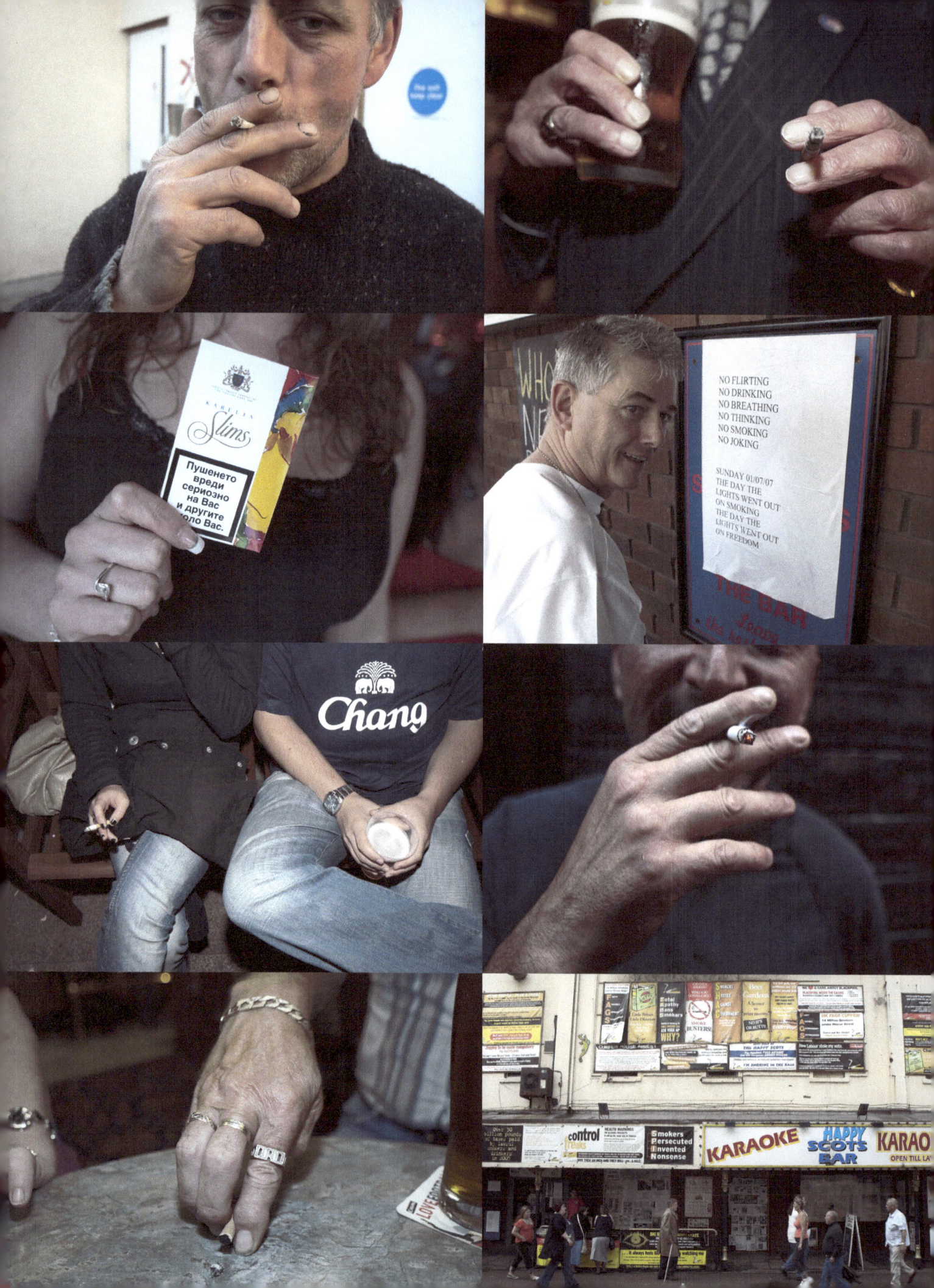

THE last day to legally smoke in public places in England – trawling the pubs of Preston, Lancashire, capturing smokers doing their thing.

There were some very accommodating people along the way. Some were happy to let me photograph them, some were genuinely interested in what I was doing, some played up to the camera.

Occasionally you get a negative reaction from people when you approach them with a camera. They can be quite abusive. So when you get kind words and polite conversation it makes your job easier and is very much appreciated.

My only wish after Saturday night is that I don't meet the foul-mouthed young lady I took a photo of in The Old Bull again.

'Take my picture, now f*** off', she said. Charming. Just the sort of girl you'd want to introduce to your parents.

It was a grueling night. I allowed myself a ten-minute break and a pint of Guinness in Preston's finest pub, the Black Horse, before carrying on with the snapping.

These are the pubs which kindly allowed me to photograph on their premises: The Blue Bell, Old Dog Inn, The Academy, Yates, The Old Bull, The Wellington, the Stanley Arms, the Black-a-Moor, the Market Tavern, the Black Horse, the New Britannia, Roper Hall, O'Neills and the Adelphi.

But the project didn't end on Saturday night. At 10.45am on Sunday morning I was at Happy Scots Bar in Blackpool for England's first illegal 'smoke-in'. I was made incredibly welcome by owner Hamish Howitt and his pub full of defiant smokers.

Hamish's story is quite remarkable. He opposes the ban on moral grounds and has spent thousands of pounds fighting it – even registering a slightly misleadingly-named political party, UK Fags, to battle the ban. All the major TV channels were there – this sort of stuff is TV gold, especially for a slow Sunday newsday.

Hamish, who does not smoke, was prepared to go to jail for his cause.

The pub was packed with all walks of life, from teenagers to war veterans. Some people supporting the fight didn't even smoke and some of those had their first fag in 20 years.

June 30, 2007

30/6

Hanging fire until
the doors open tomorrow:
disassembled coughs,
some good jokes
and some bad,
your politics,
my drunken disposition.

Some disagreements
and the odd shout.
The bounced remains
of a sudden exclamation,
some important and
some inconsequential words,
a few promises and curses.

The chairs are upended
and the butts swept away.
Then the ashtrays washed
and stashed in a box with
the scold's bridle and the
bear's harness.

This new day,
as the doors open,
an era dissolves into the street;
leaving the smell of beer
and sweat
and piss.

Steve Rouse

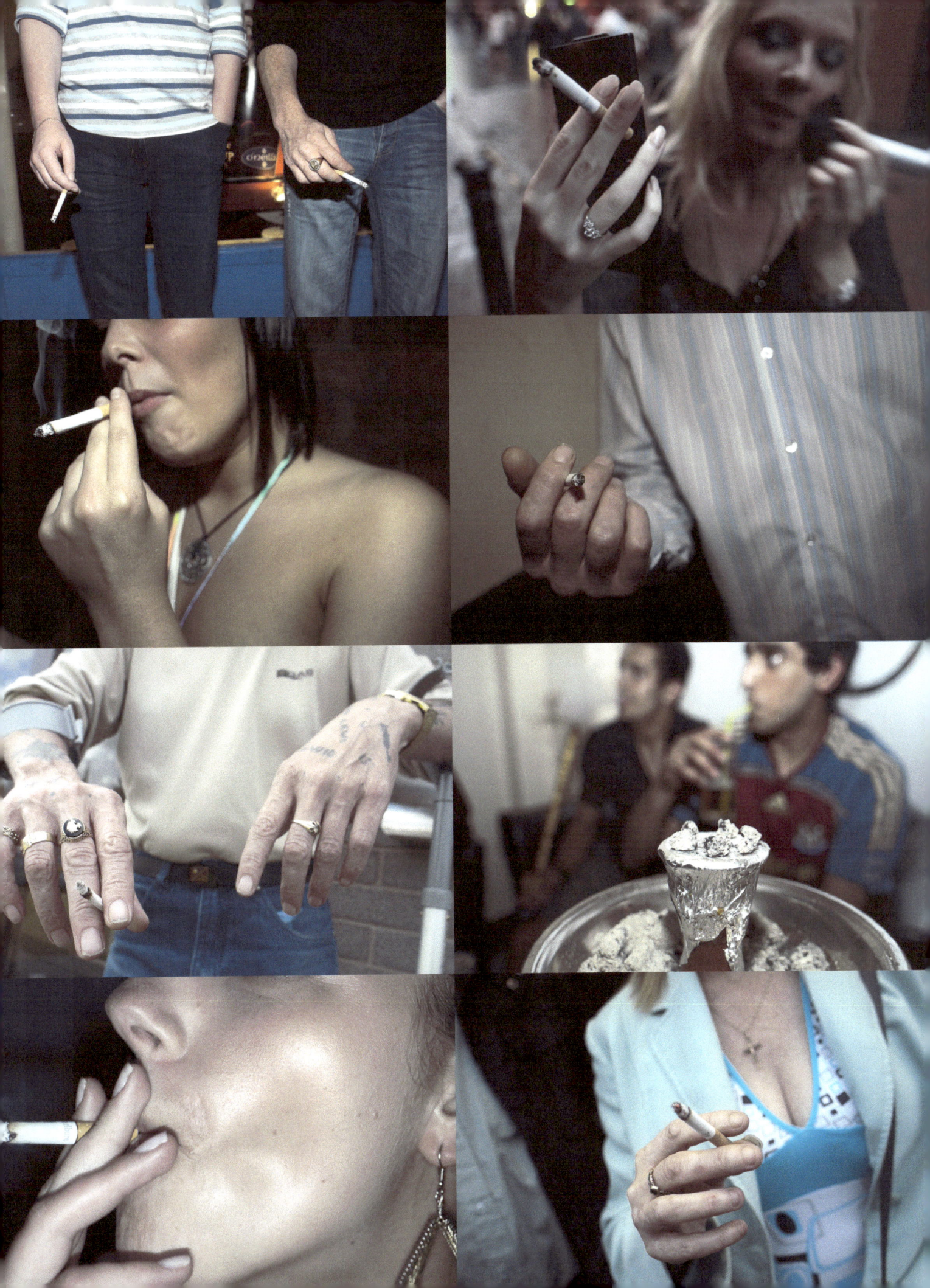

'UNLUCKY. F*** off.' It was gruff voice uttering these words with no small amount of aggression. That was one bloke's response to my request to photograph him and his wife down the side of a Preston pub (O'Neill's if you must know). He was crouching down at the time. Didn't even turn his head towards me.

His wife, who seemed quite reasonable, immediately tut-tutted at her husband. I adopted my calmest, sympathetic voice and said, 'okay, no problem, but you don't have to be so rude' before walking away to the noise of the couple arguing.

He had stood up by this point, chest was puffed out as he eyeballed me. She must be so proud of her Alpha Male. What a nice man!

August 12, 2007

IN recent weeks I've been to Preston, Blackpool, Manchester and Liverpool, all the time roaming for smokers.

I think I have been right in going for lots of flash and a snap-shot approach. Attention spans of the drunk can be very short, I'm taking over 200 pictures a night and, of course, it's dark. Ask a drunk person if you can take his photograph and all of a sudden his 15 friends appear for the group shop you didn't want. I think these pictures will say as much about alcohol as they do about smoking.

If these images are lacking in aesthetic beauty they do display vivid colours and harsh light to give a brash reality the subject.

These pictures are not about seduction. I noticed in my research how many photographers had produced smoke-related photographs of beauty. This was done for no other reason than juxtaposition; showing something so dirty as a cigarette as a thing of beauty. None of that here.

Photographs work best if they show a contrast, even more so if they include irony. But do they mean anything beyond their basic cleverness?

Some people look stupid in my photographs. Is that my fault? It's not deliberate.

I've also seen more mooning men's arses than I would care to. Why do some people understand 'take your photograph' as 'drop trousers and pull a moonie'? And it's never the women either.

September 3, 2007

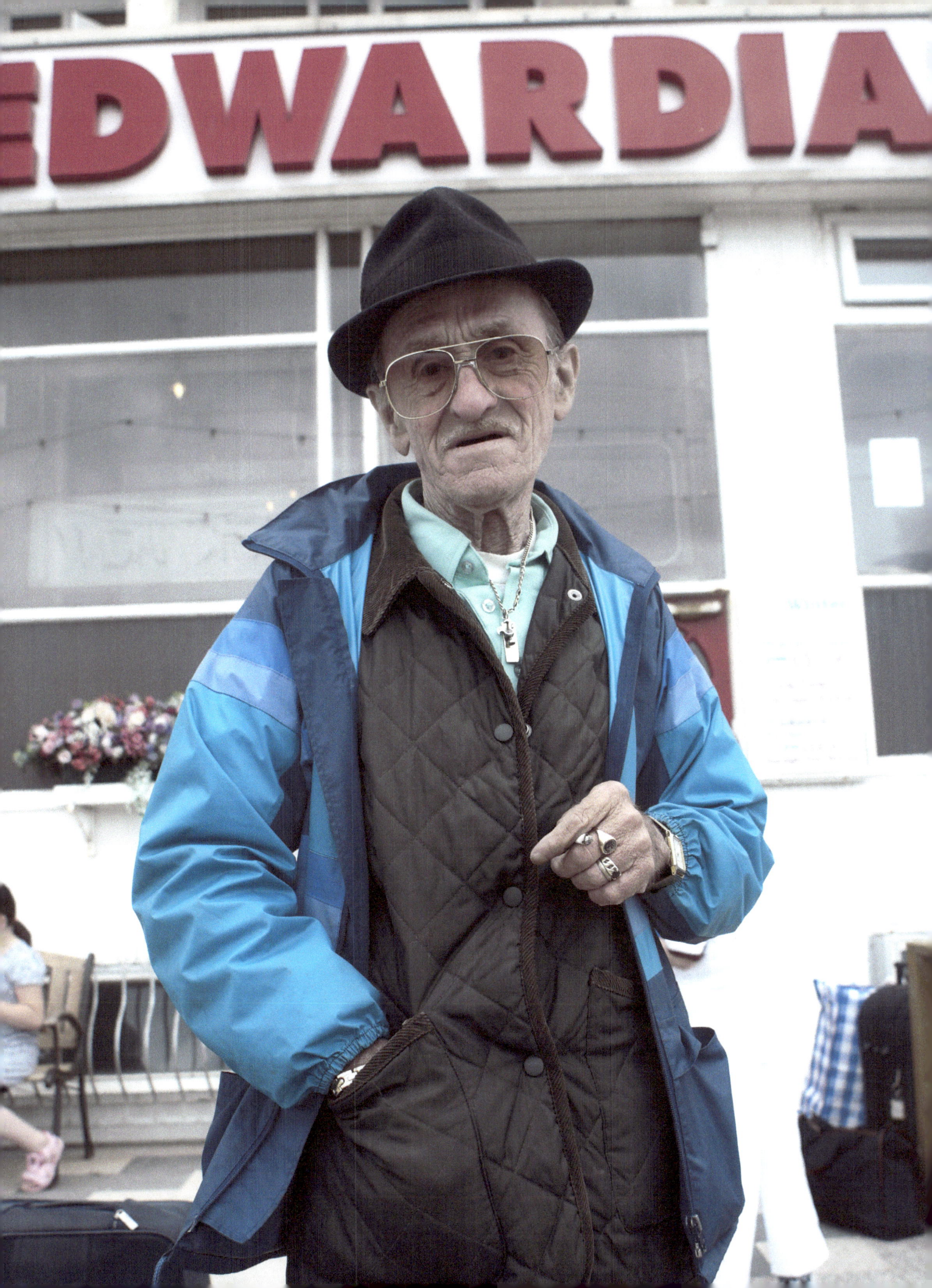

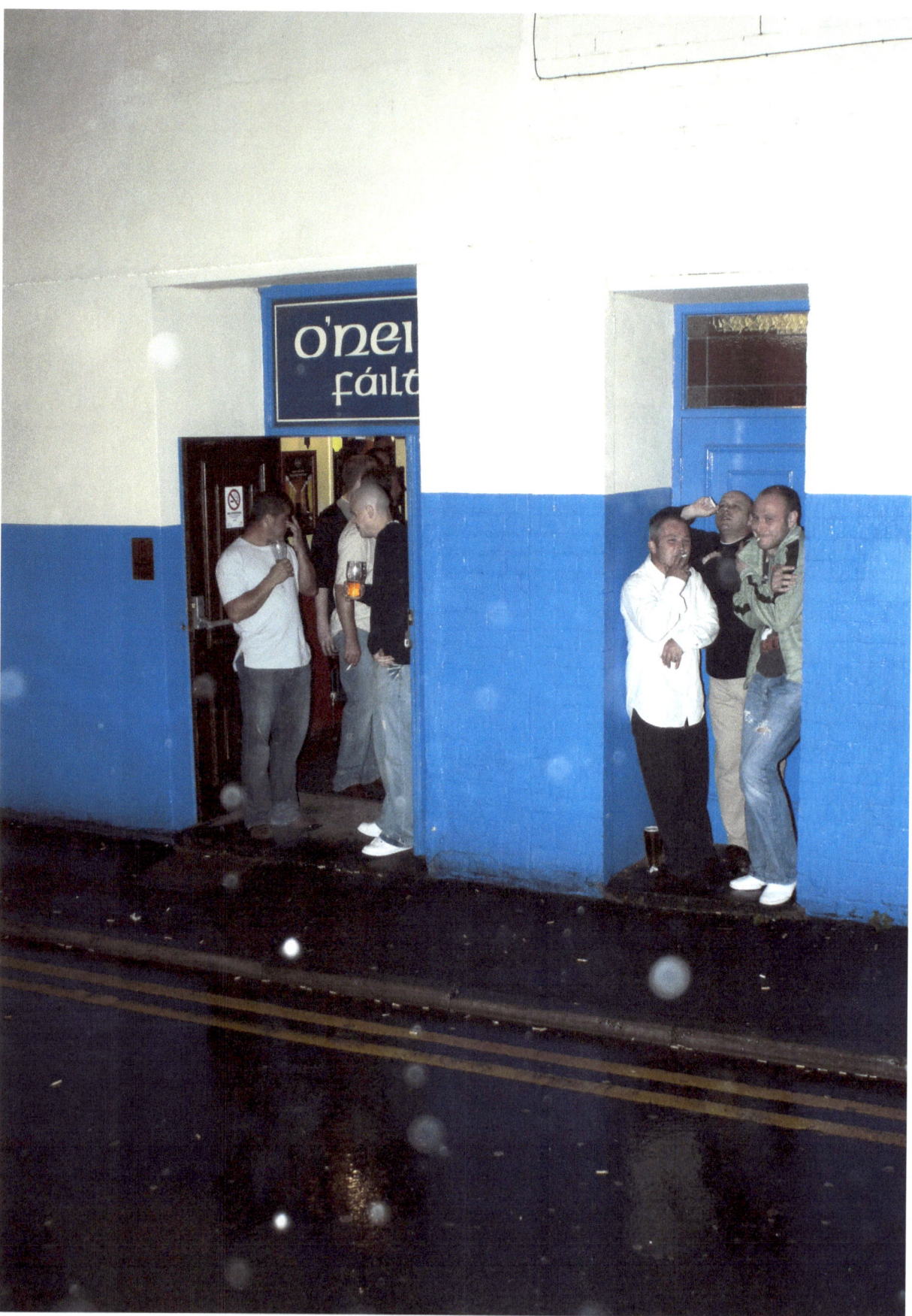

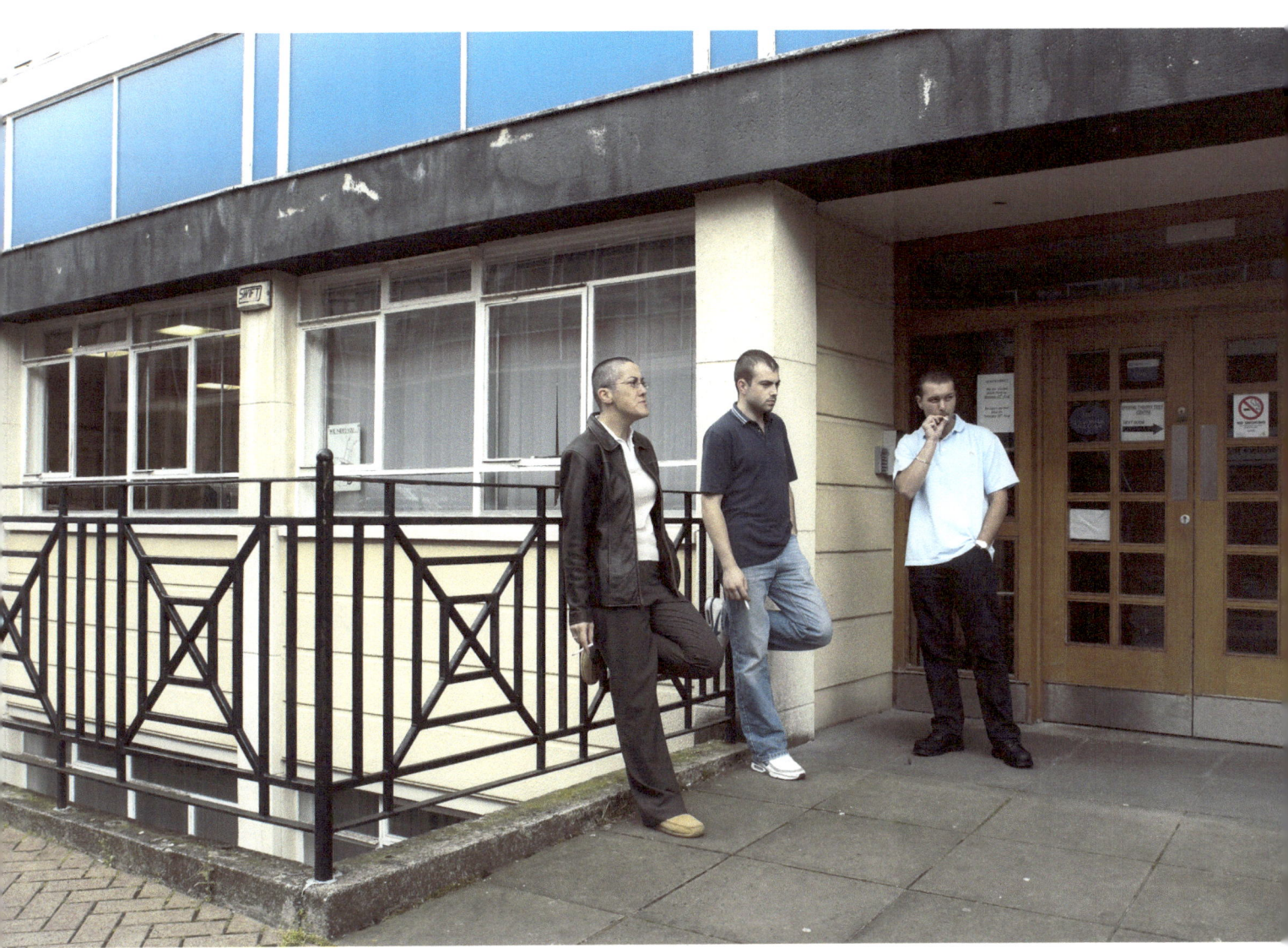

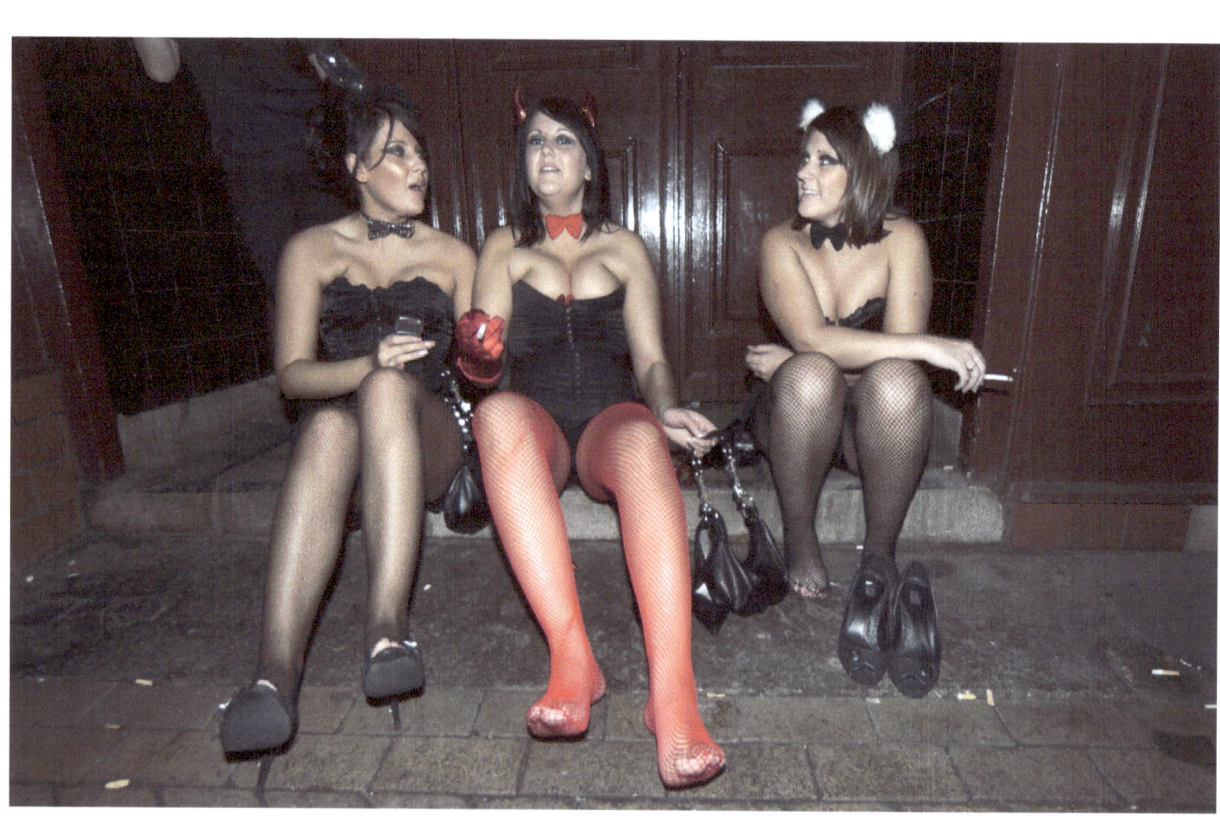

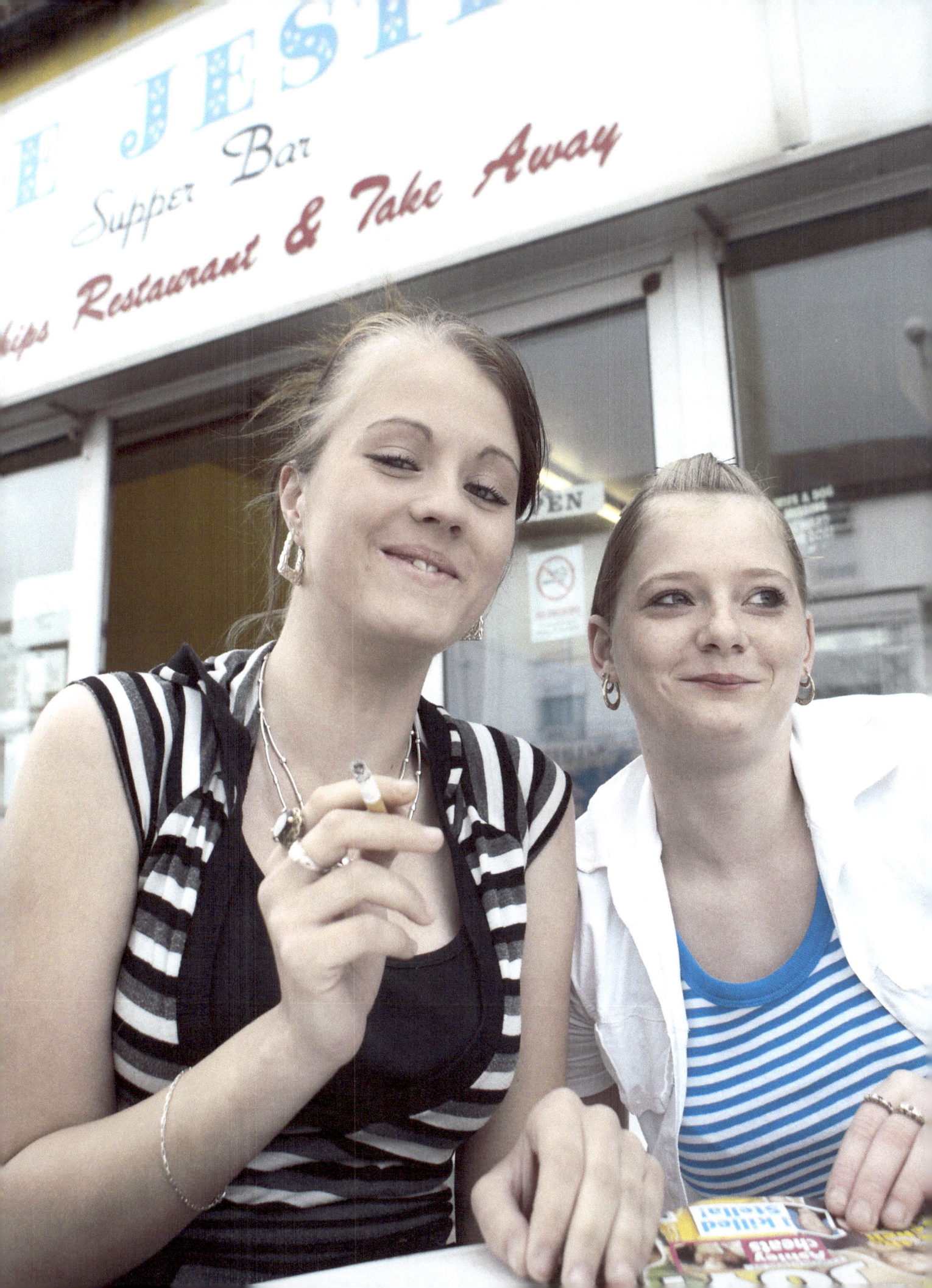

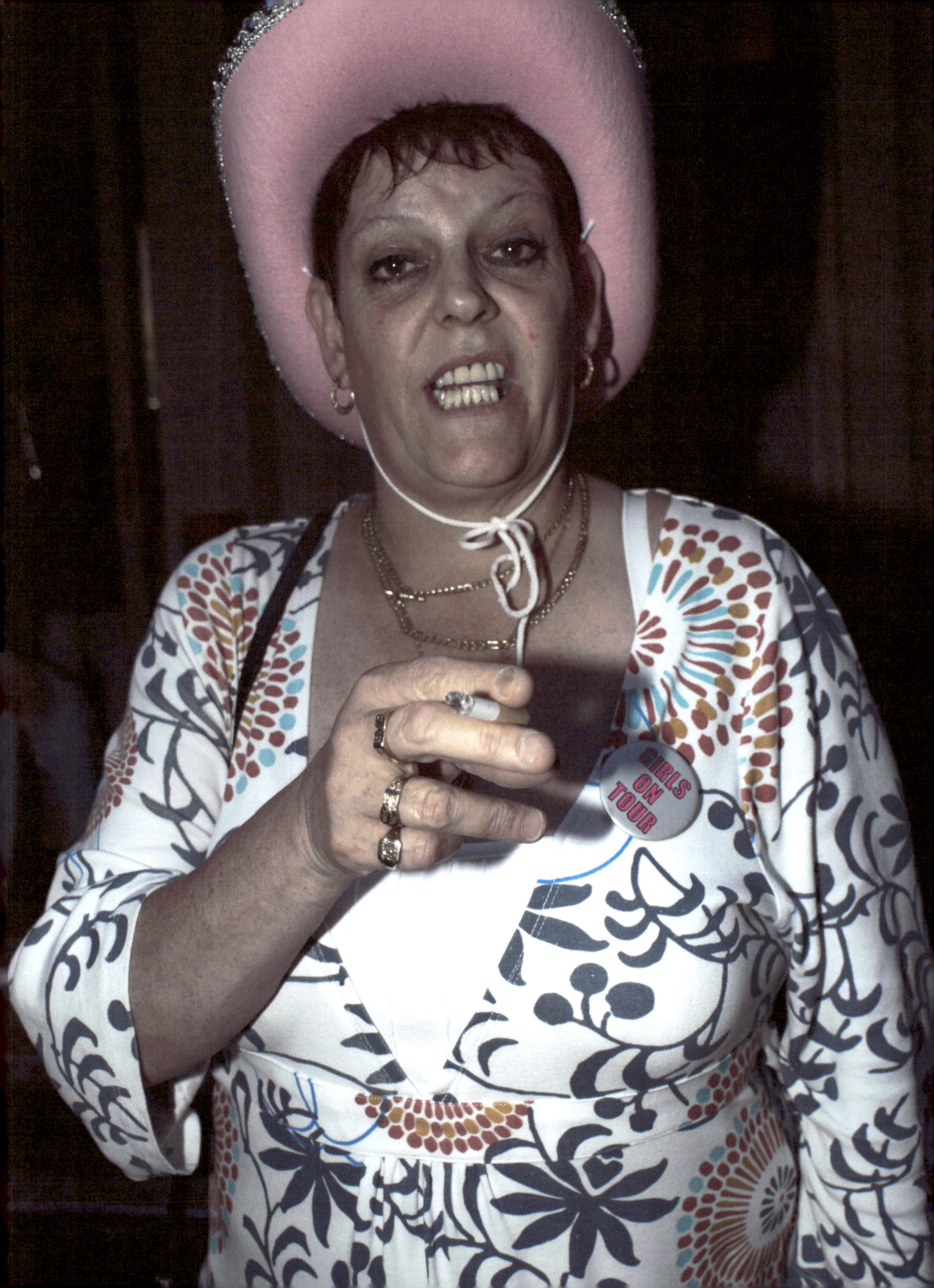

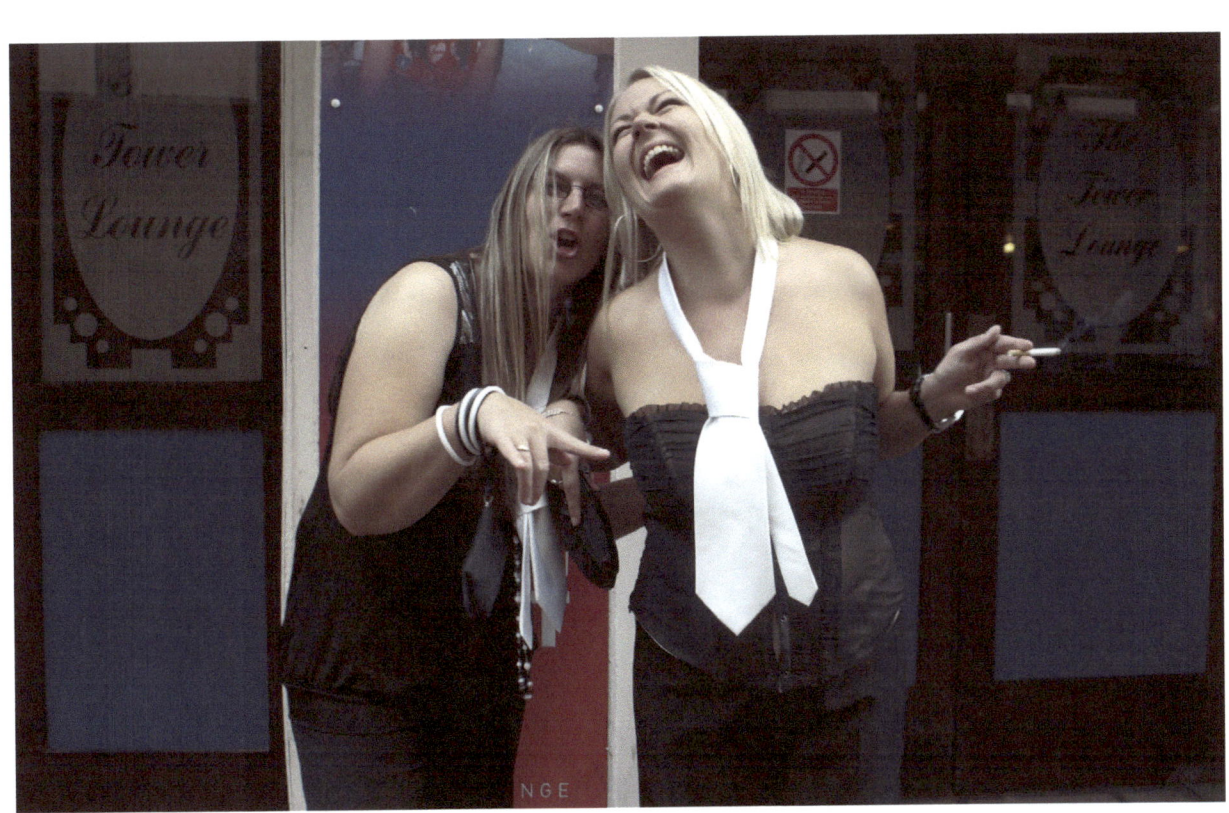

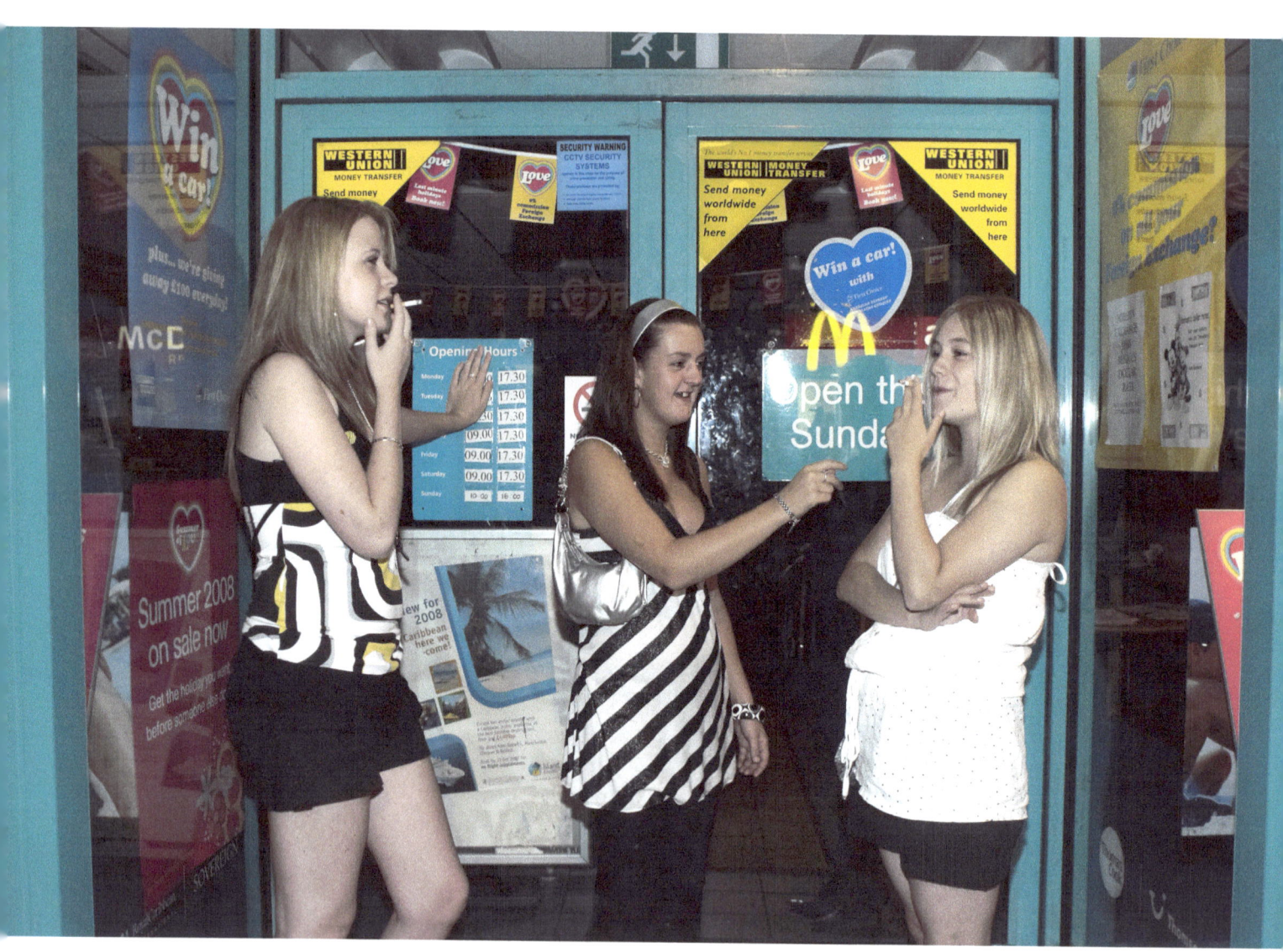

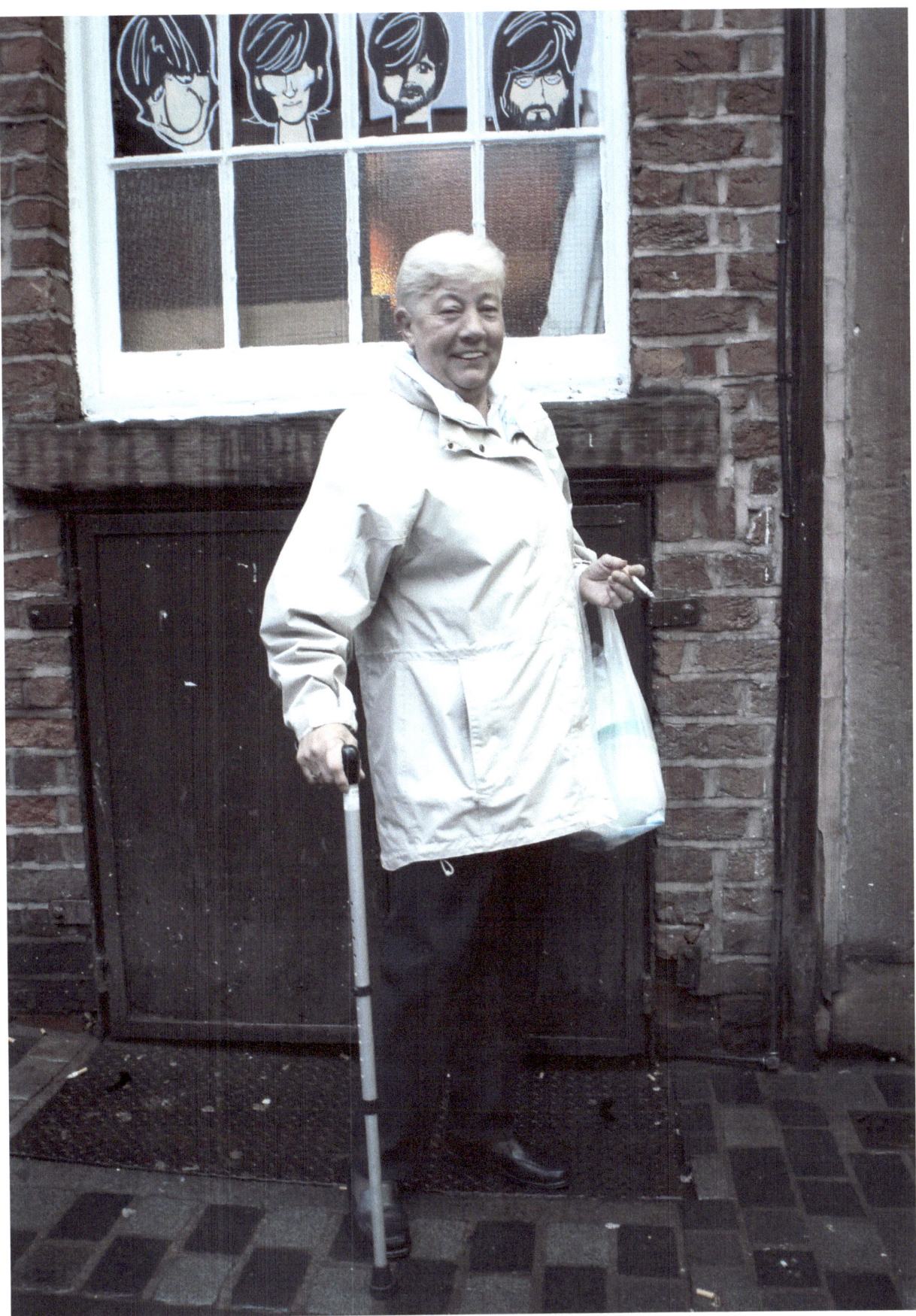

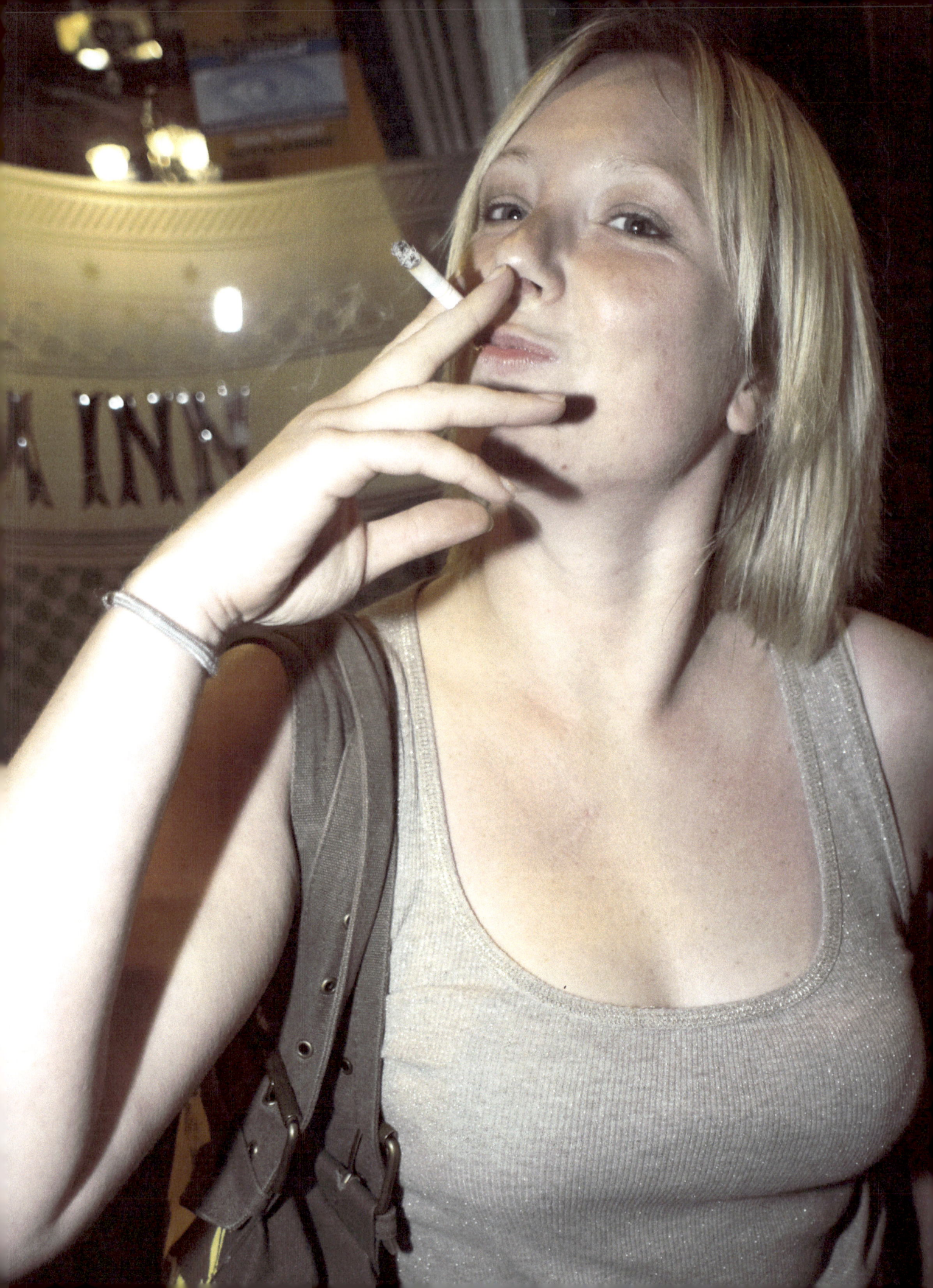

I WAS not expecting much joy from Deansgate in Manchester, where all the posh bars have street tables and chairs. I got a couple of negative responses before things started to take off. People were watching and listening as I persuaded one table to allow me to photograph them. Then, as I left, it was 'aren't you going to photograph us?' It snowballed from there.

There are a lot of bouncers outside the Deansgate bars and quite a few wanted to know what I was doing, but none stopped me photographing.

It was the same story down Oxford Road. The moshers and the hen parties were only too happy to oblige. As were the inhabitants of Canal Street.

After a stop off at a pub in Walkden, Worsley, it was back up the M61 to Preston.

Two targets here: the smokers section of Lava Ignite nightclub (Tokyo Jo's to me) and outside Squires nightclub where the smokers must stand in a rather exposed pen.

I was denied permission to photograph here as the manageress (who has been supportive in the past) was off and her deputy said she was unable to grant me permission. Strictly speaking this is not true as the smokers pen is on the street, but it's silly to do these things without co-operation.

It was surreal in the smokers area of Lava Ignite where the punters have to queue to get in the 6ft by 12ft walled in area. Queuing to get into a smoking area? Barmy.

It got a bit mental. It was around 11pm and people were very drunk. There were a lot of requests for me to take photographs without anyone caring about what I was doing.

In the Old Dog Inn I got talking to a rather delightful couple who attend fetish nights in Preston. Had no idea there was one held in Bitter Suite once a month. Sounded very interesting. 'They are,' she said, 'especially in the dark corners.' 'Can I come along?' I asked. She nodded. 'Can I take photographs?' 'You'll get your throat cut', she replied. I'll take that as a no.

October 3, 2007

IN DOORWAYS

Slowly it shortens as orange burns to grey
while rested between middle and index finger
Lift filter-tip to mouth, blow a tiny ash cloud
during ten-minute breaks from the world inside

Cluster in doorways for this habitual pause
It's no longer as natural as a phone call or pint
Take a deep breath, as the atmosphere's changed
then meet fresh air with fire, as if no one can see

Lend a light to a friend crossed on the back stairs
Let charred endings fall on to pavement and glass
See Government warnings on the pack of 20
and weigh up word blindness or nicotine gum

Discard butts in unison and crush with heels
as if killing a moment before returning indoors
Feel satisfied for now, life's OK like this
Slowly it shortens as light burns to grey.

MIKE WHALLEY

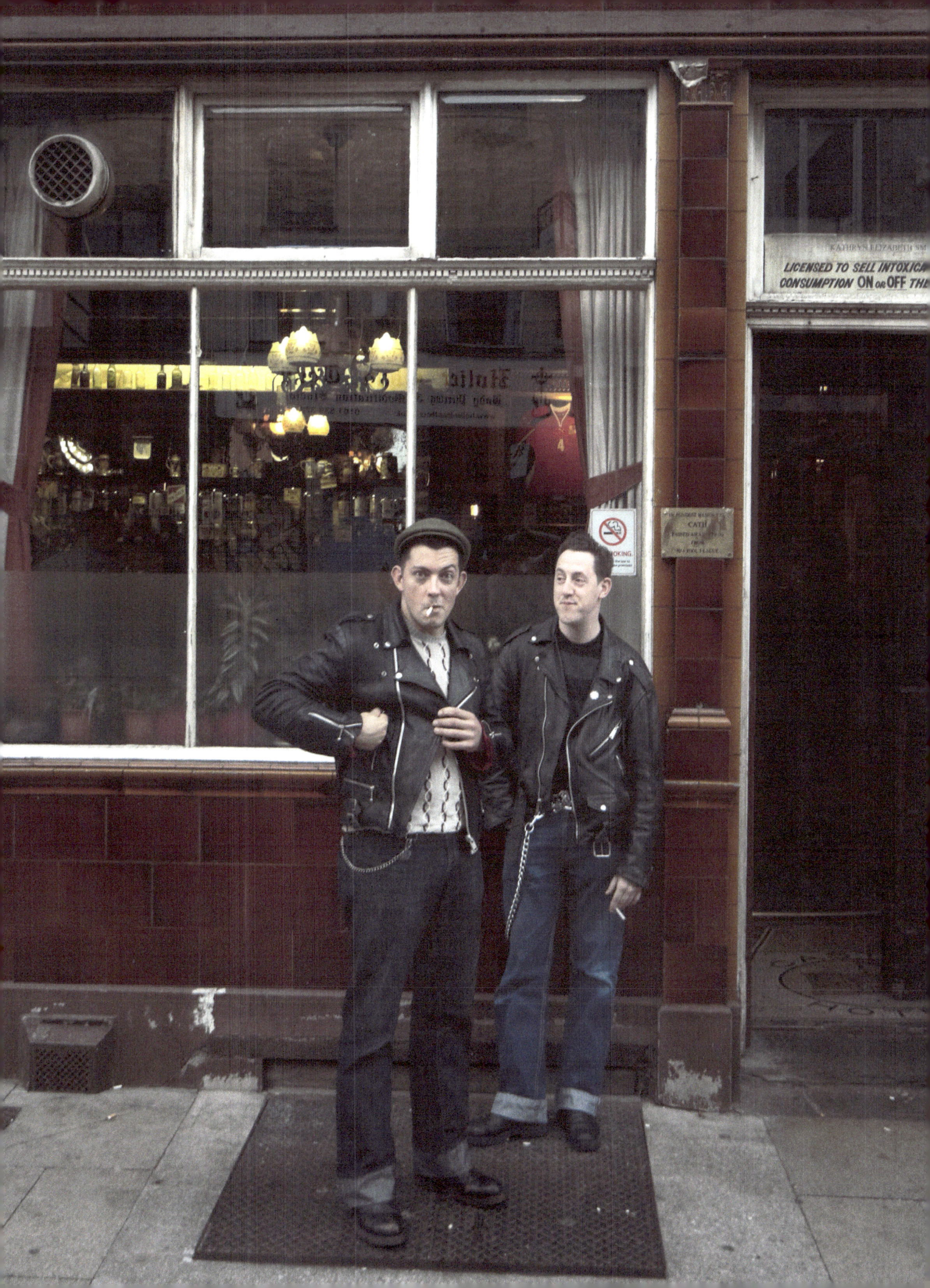

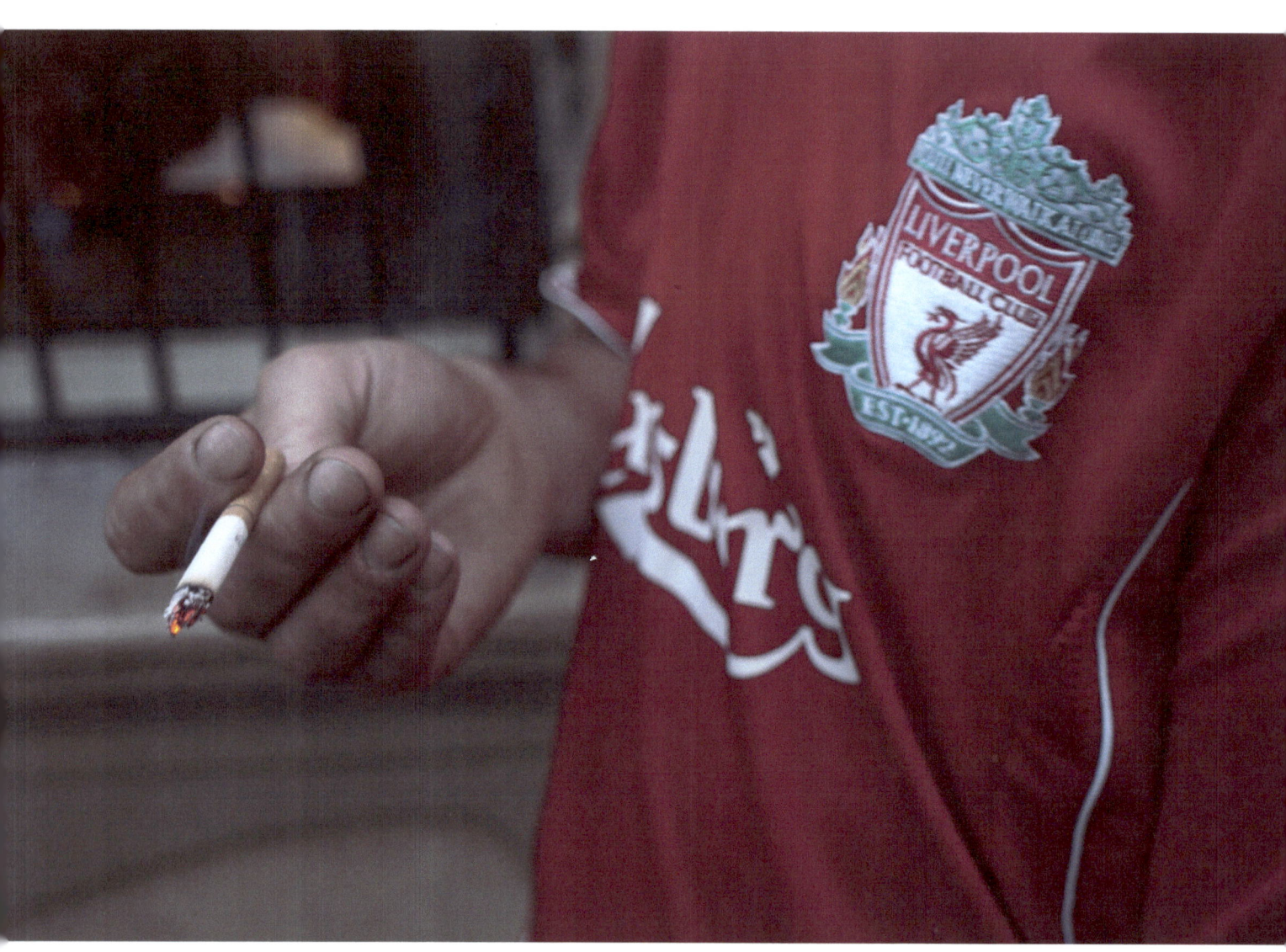

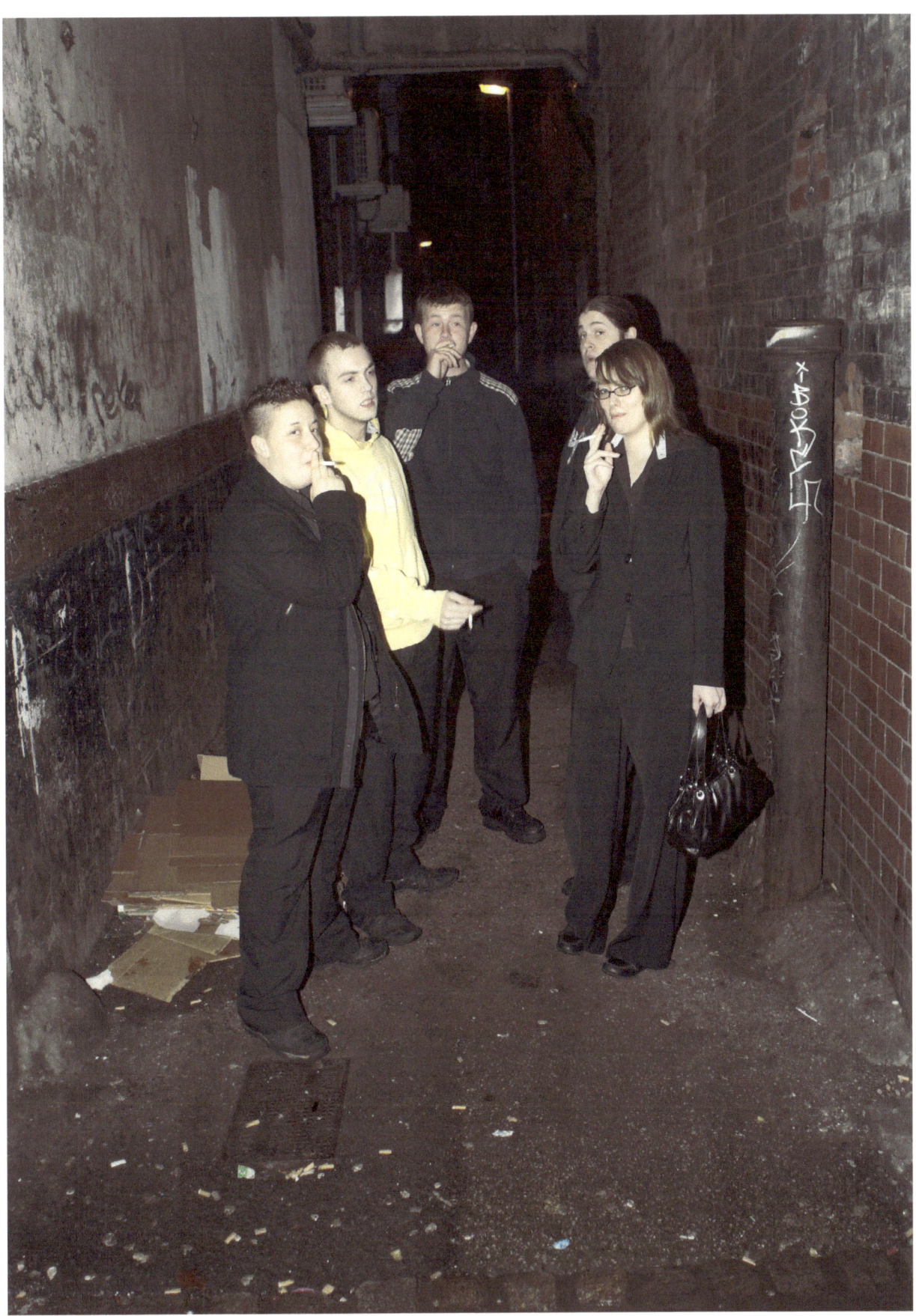

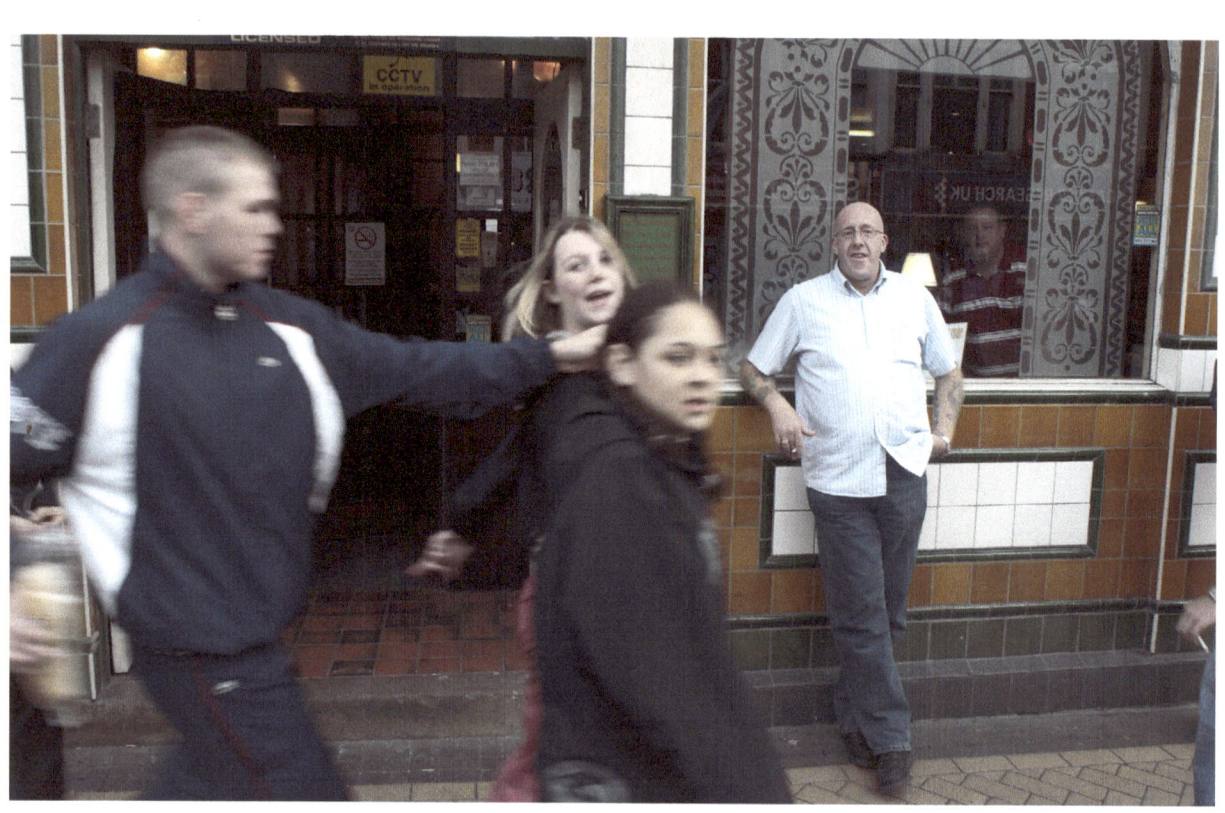

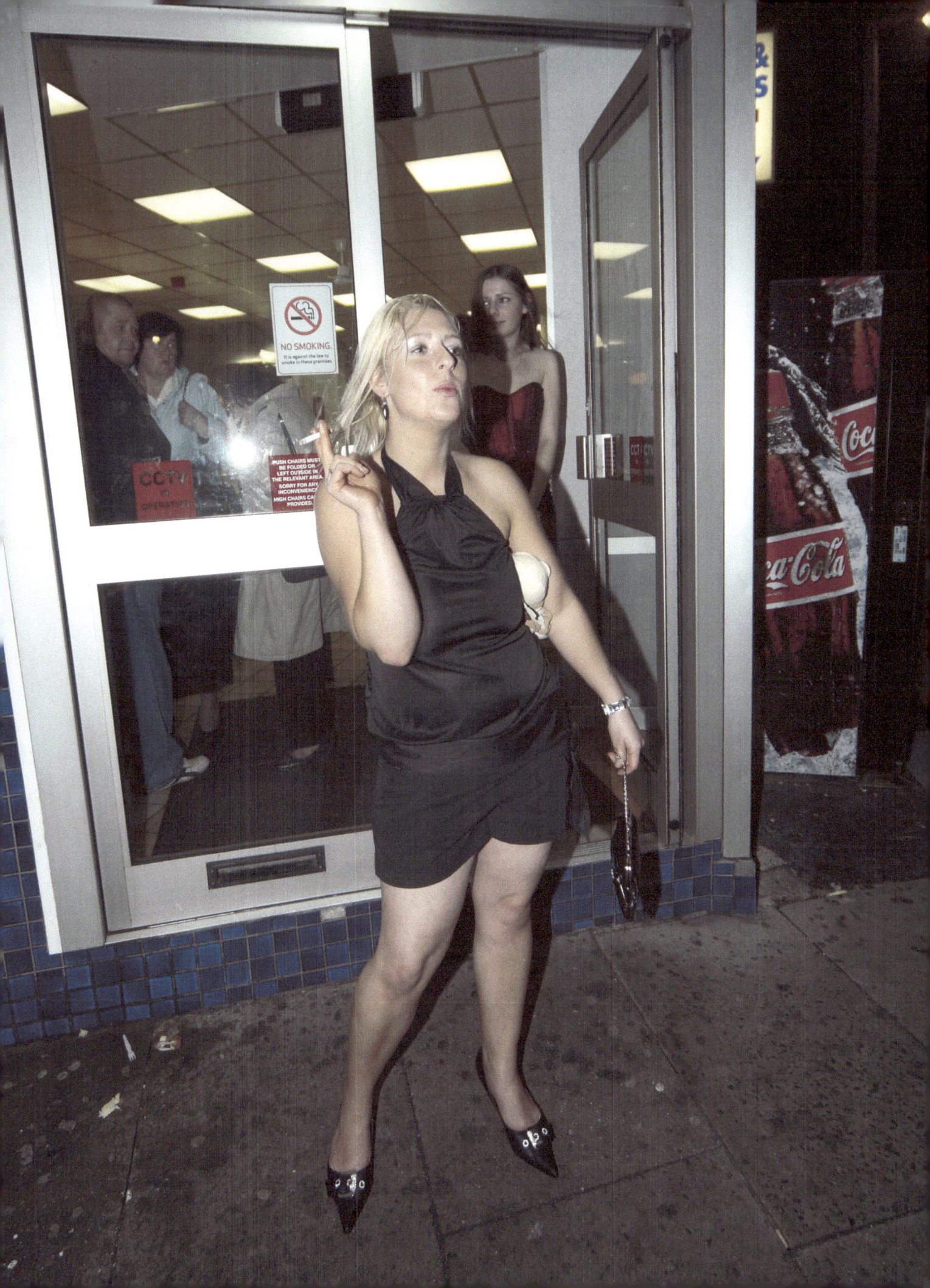

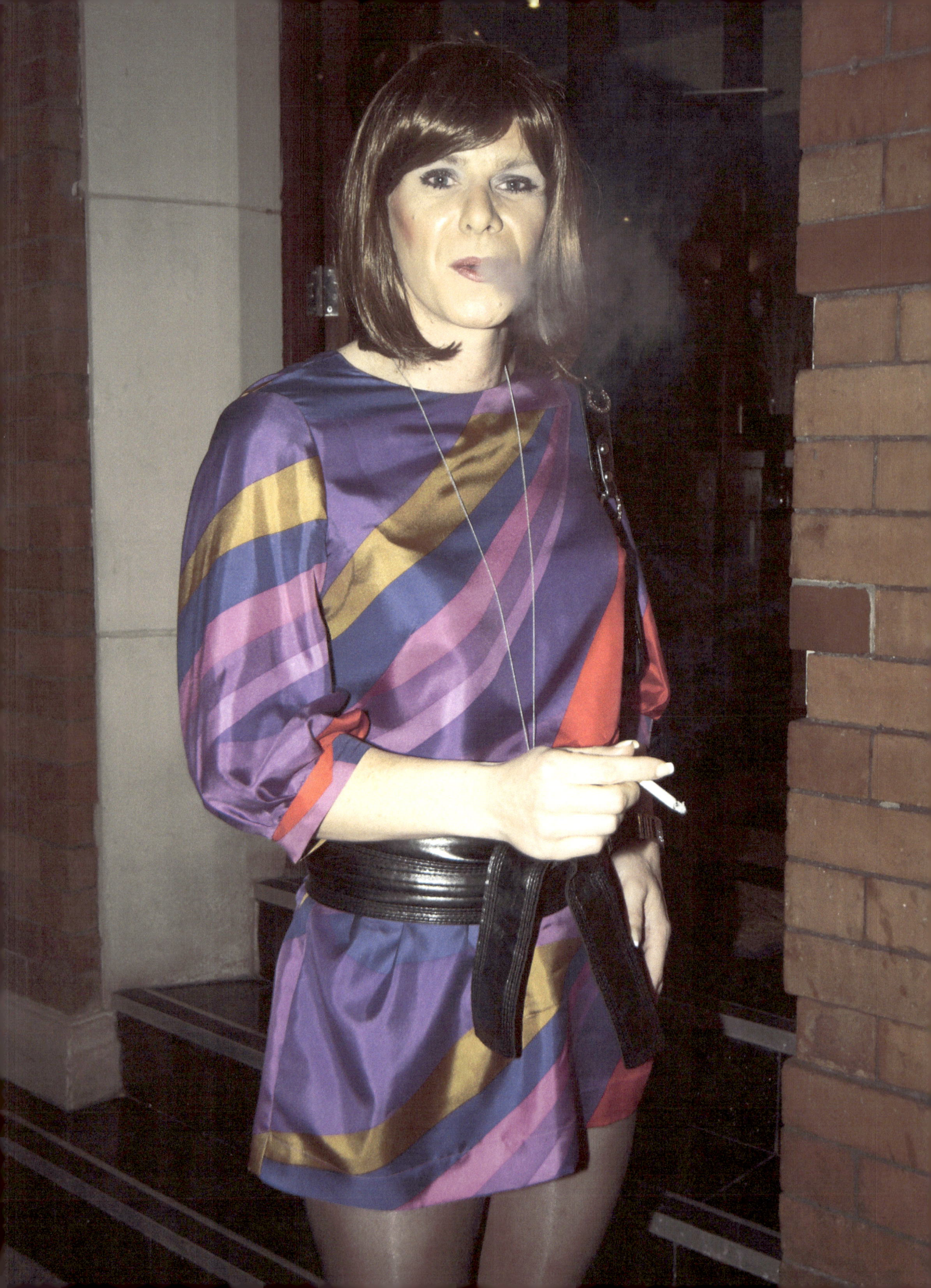

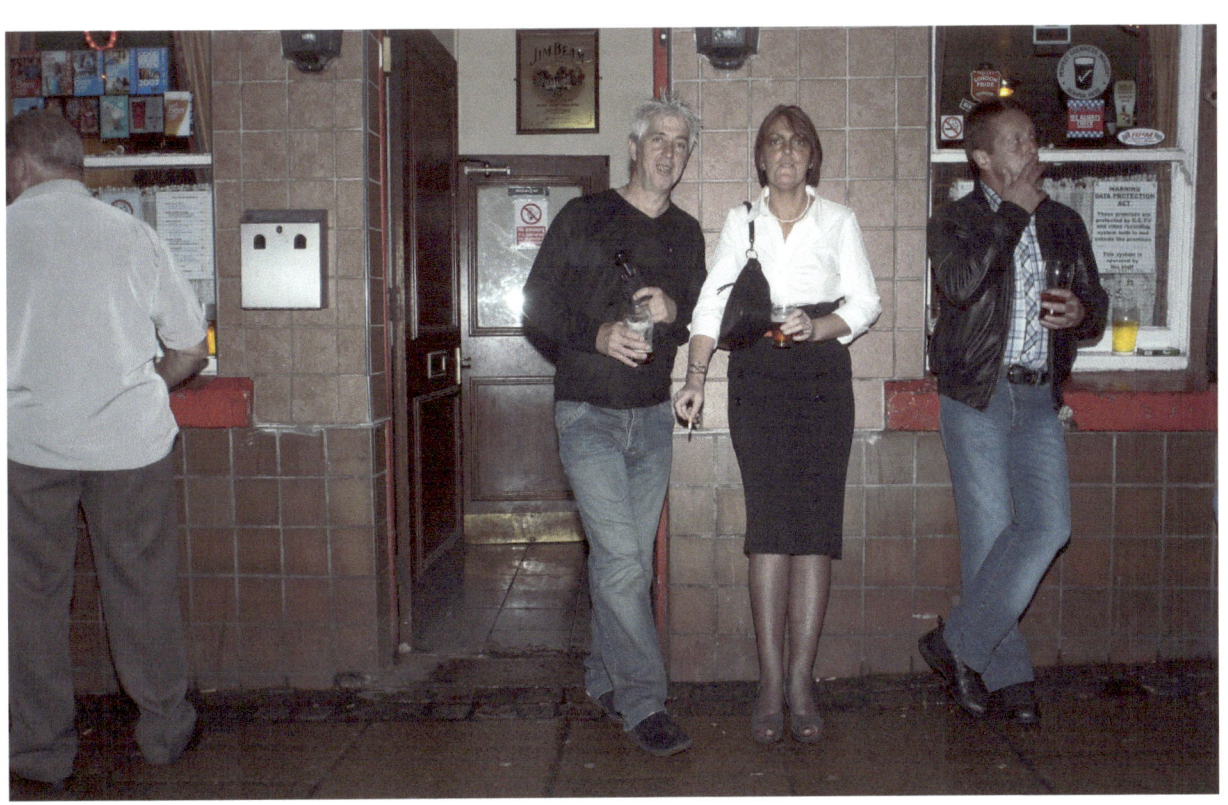

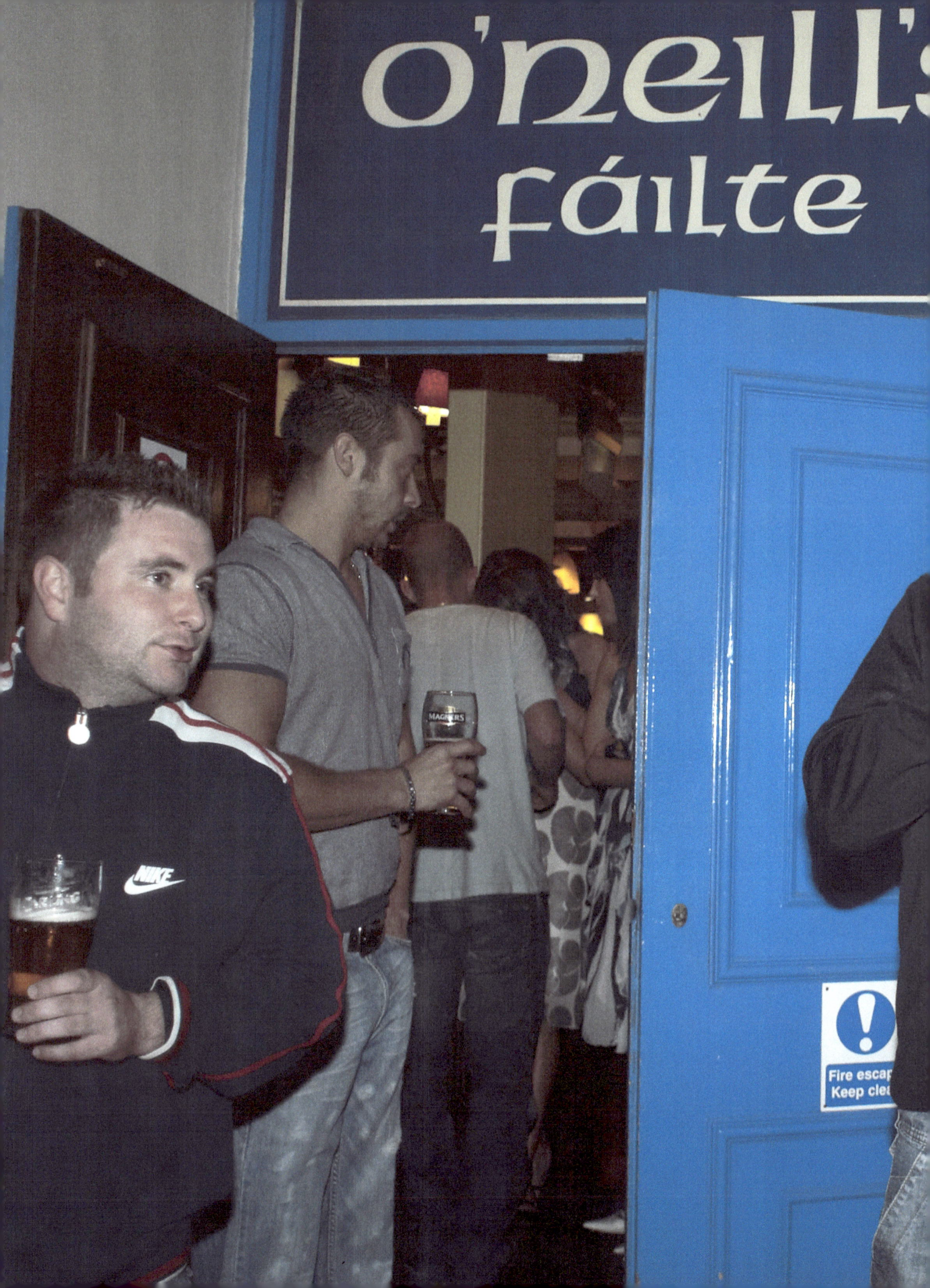

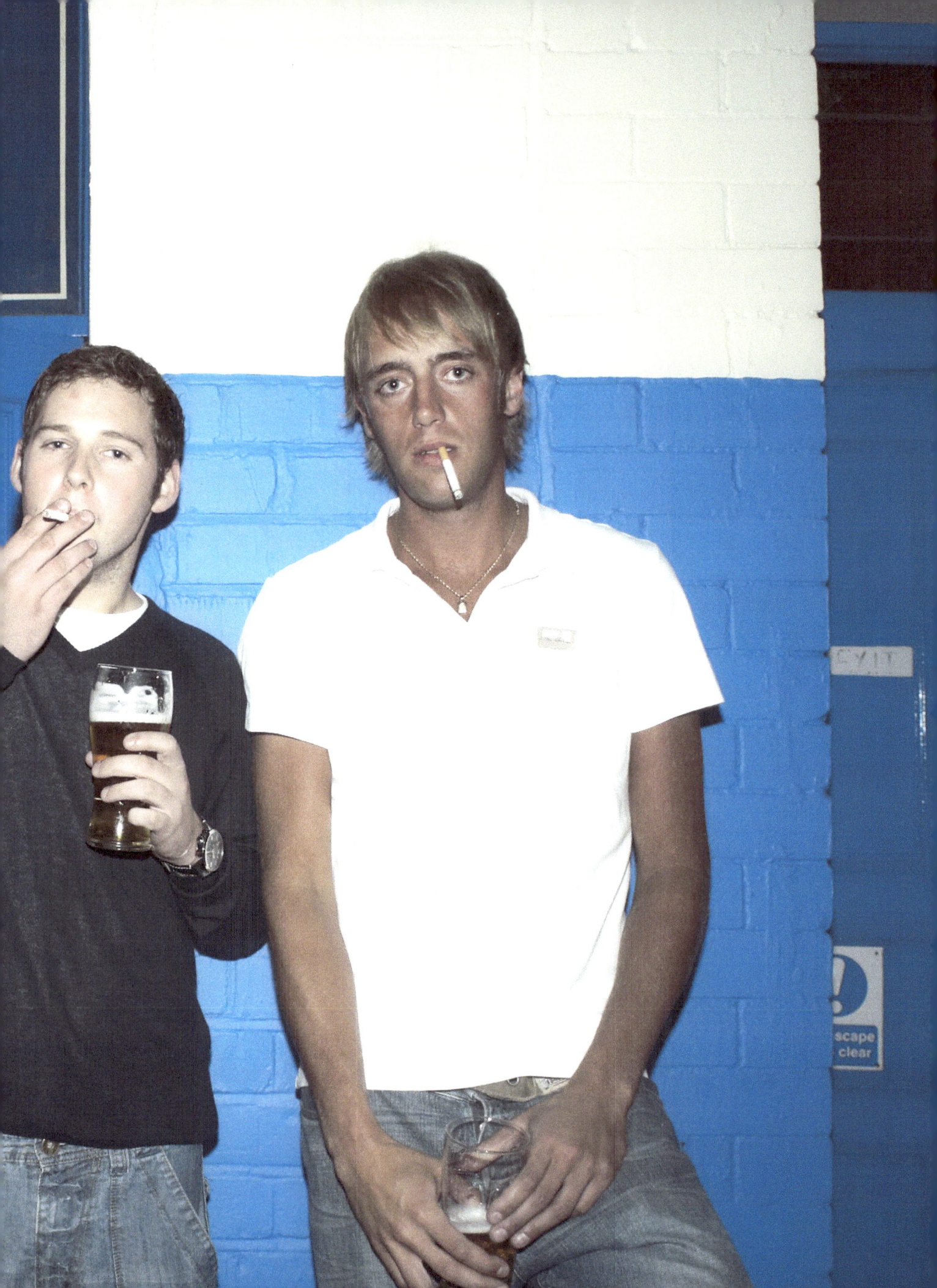

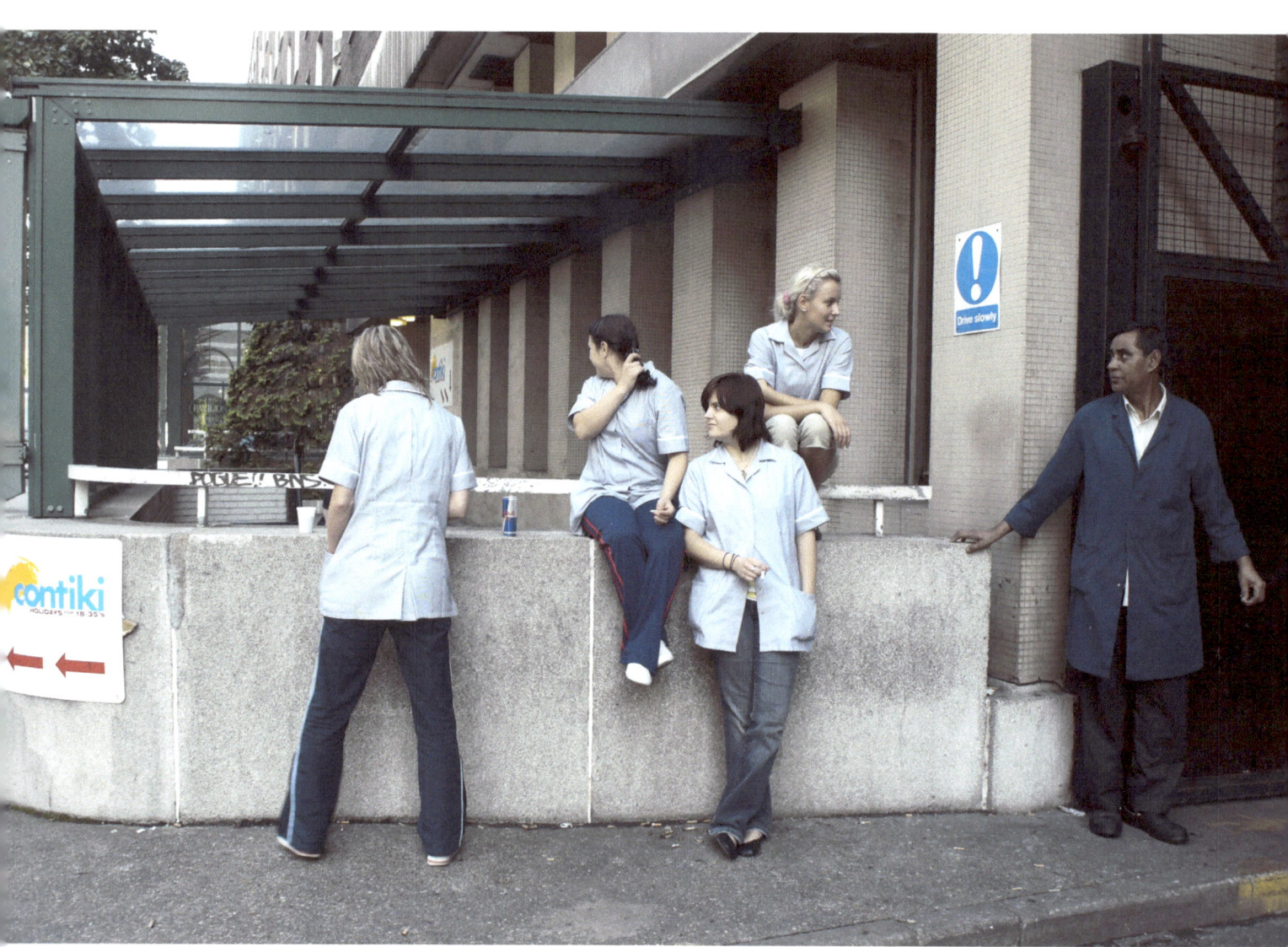

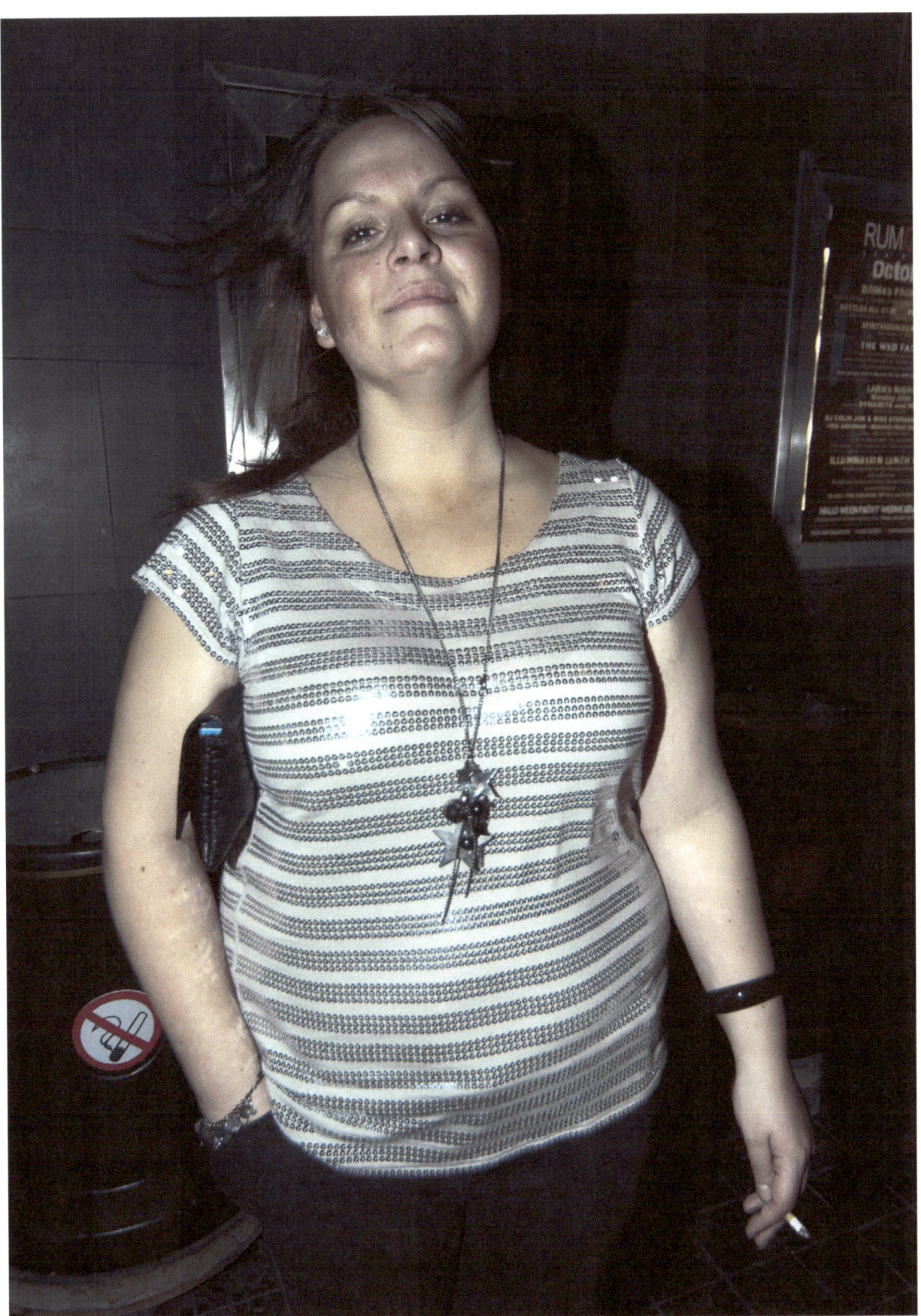

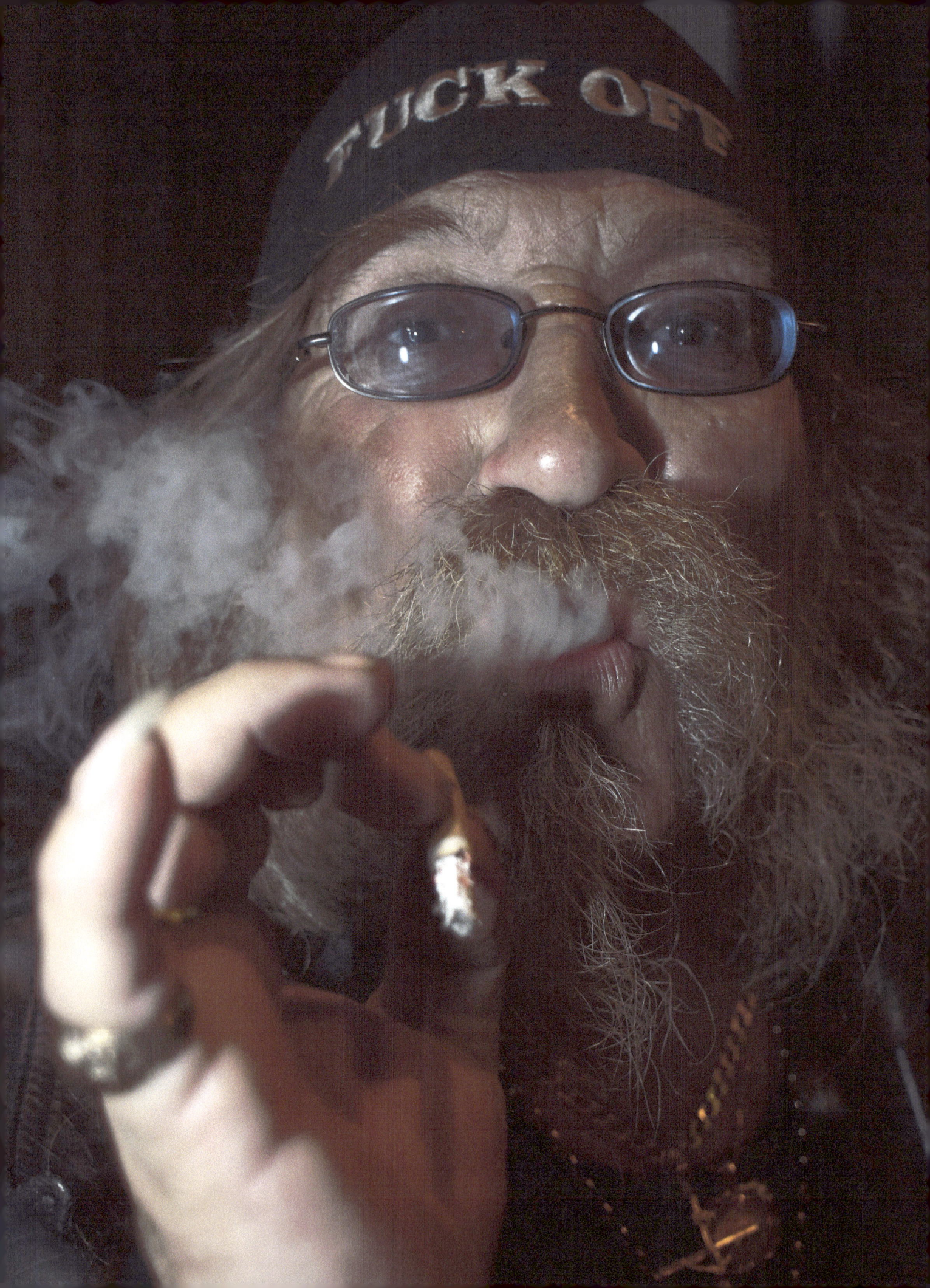

MY last night taking smoking pictures, just a week before November 5 when Blackpool's famous Illuminations go dark.

I wanted to get some Illuminations shots before I hit the pubs – but it was raining and very windy. I ended up wasting a couple of hours. Nevermind.

I was looking to get more portraits. I did get a couple. But I'd like to pay my respects to the lass with the orange hands from Yorkshire (Barnsley or Doncaster – I can't remember). I bumped into her outside the chippy. Then there was the shoeless bunny girl with the panda eyes sitting on the step outside resort's famous Tower Lounge. 'What? You want to take a photo of me looking like this?' she asked, as sweat dripped down the side of her make-up smudged face. I don't need to answer that question, do I?

October 28, 2007

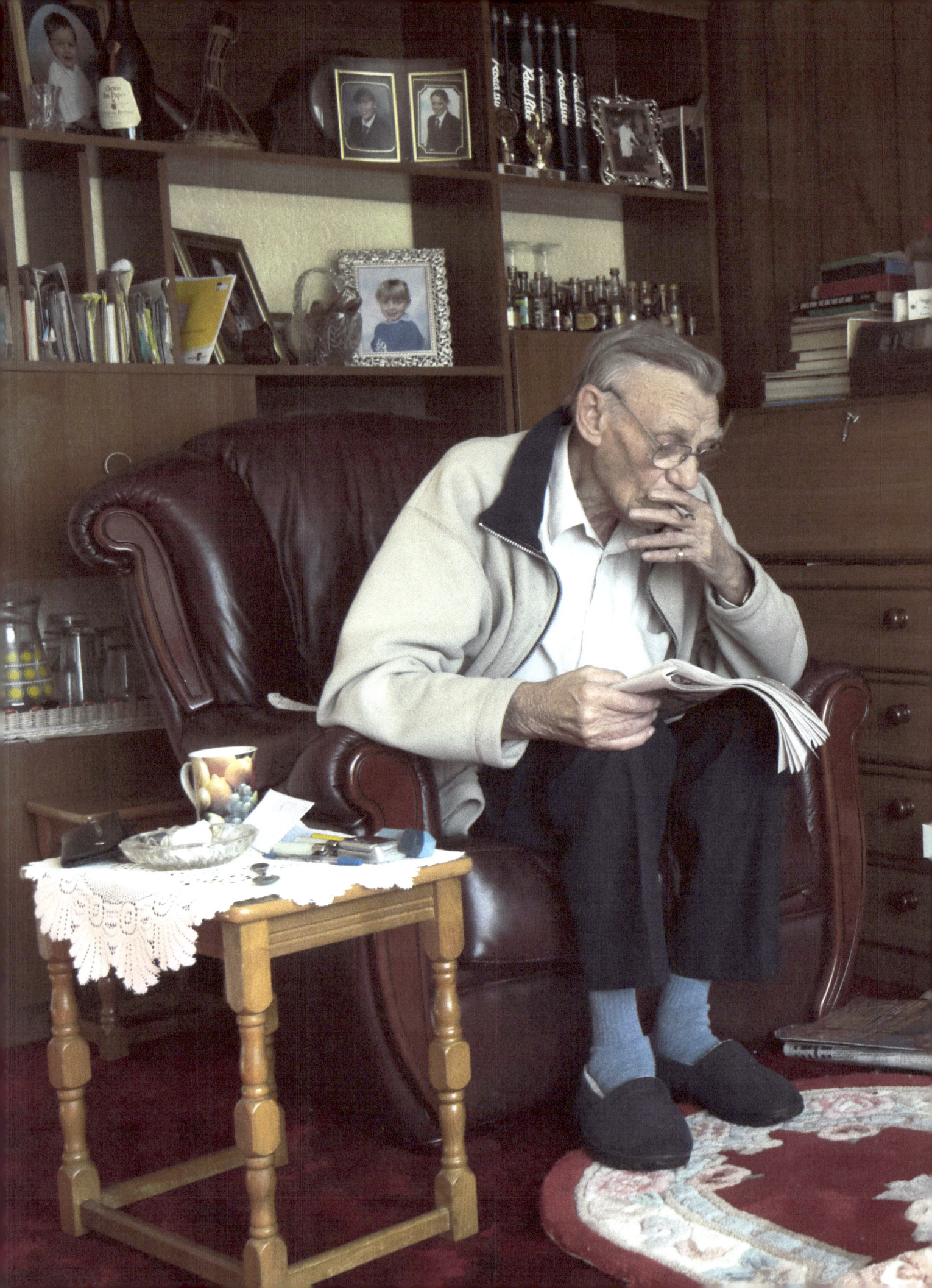

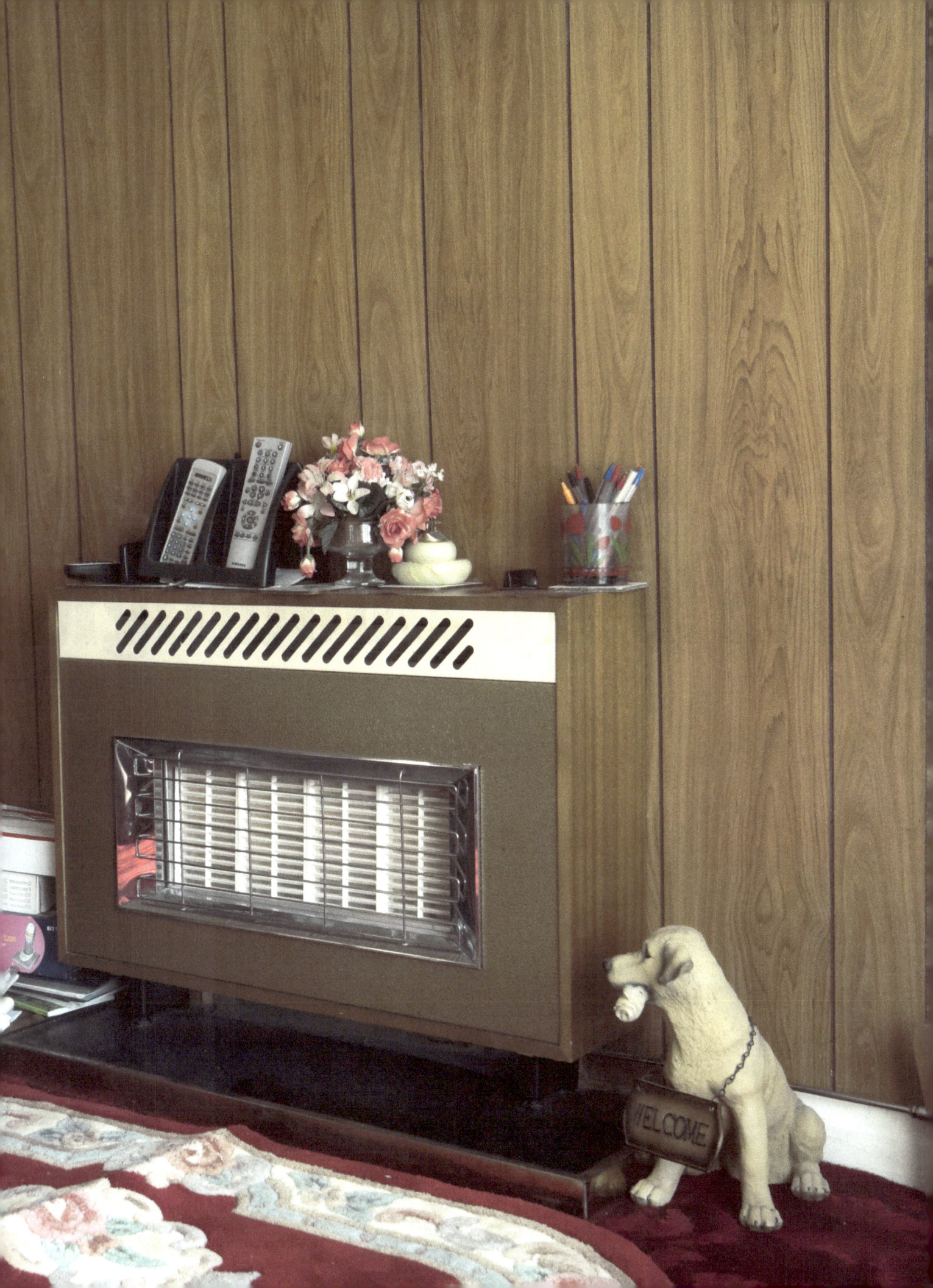

The End
Marlboro Goodnight

Thanks to all those who agreed to be photographed, especially dad's Uncle Ernie, sadly no longer with us.
Thanks to poets Mike Whalley, for his specially commisioned prose In Doorways, and Steve Rouse for 30/6.
And also a round of applause to Rob Mager and his band Midnight Mafia who wrote the song
The Smoke Has Gone for this project (which you can't hear in this book).

www.ingramcontent.com/pod-product-compliance
Lightning Source LLC
Chambersburg PA
CBHW051047180526
45172CB00002B/547

978 1477 608142